SpringerBriefs in Computer Science

For further volumes:
http://www.springer.com/series/10028

Lingyu Wang • Massimiliano Albanese
Sushil Jajodia

Network Hardening

An Automated Approach to Improving Network Security

 Springer

Lingyu Wang
Concordia Institute for Information
    Systems Engineering (CIISE)
Concordia University
Montreal, QC, Canada

Massimiliano Albanese
Center for Secure Information Systems
George Mason University
Fairfax, VA, USA

Sushil Jajodia
Center for Secure Information Systems
George Mason University
Fairfax, VA, USA

ISSN 2191-5768   ISSN 2191-5776 (electronic)
ISBN 978-3-319-04611-2 ISBN 978-3-319-04612-9 (eBook)
DOI 10.1007/978-3-319-04612-9
Springer Cham Heidelberg New York Dordrecht London

Library of Congress Control Number: 2014932046

Printed on acid-free paper

Springer is part of Springer Science+Business Media (www.springer.com)

Acknowledgements

This research was funded in part by the US Army Research Office under grants W911NF-13-1-0421, W911NF-09-1-0525, and W911NF-11-1-0340; by the Office of Naval Research under grants N00014-12-1-0461 and N00014-13-1-0703; by the National Institutes of Standard and Technology under grant 70NANB12H236; and by the Natural Sciences and Engineering Research Council of Canada Discovery Grant N01035.

Contents

Chapter 1
Introduction

Abstract In defending networks against potential intrusions, certain vulnerabilities may seem acceptable risks when considered in isolation, whereas an intruder may combine such vulnerabilities for a multi-step intrusion and successfully infiltrate a seemingly well-guarded network. Relying on human analyst's experiences and skills to identify such a threat is error-prone and renders the task of network hardening an art, rather than a science. Existing tools based on attack graphs can reveal such threats by enumerating all possible attack paths leading to critical resources, but they cannot provide a direct solution to remove the threats. In this book, we introduce automated solutions for hardening a network against sophisticated multi-step intrusions. Specifically, we first review necessary background information on related concepts, such as attack graphs and their application to network hardening. We then describe a network hardening technique to generate hardening solutions comprised of initially satisfied conditions, which makes the solution more enforceable. Following a discussion of the complexity issues, we devise an improved technique that takes into consideration the dependencies between hardening options and employs a near-optimal approximation algorithm to scale linearly with the size of the inputs, whose performance is validated experimentally.

1.1 Background

Today's computer systems play a critical role in almost every sector of society. Such systems constitute the central component of information technology infrastructures in enterprises and in critical infrastructures including power grids, financial data systems, and emergency communication systems. Protecting these systems against network intrusions is crucial to the economy and to national security. However, the scale and severity of intrusions have continued to grow at an ever-increasing pace despite many decades of research in vulnerability analysis and intrusion detection. In this everlasting war against attackers, security researchers and administrators seem to always fall behind their opponents in technology. Firewalls and access

L. Wang et al., *Network Hardening: An Automated Approach to Improving Network Security*, SpringerBriefs in Computer Science, DOI 10.1007/978-3-319-04612-9_1,

control mechanisms may thwart intrusion attempts made by amateur attackers, but these same mechanisms can be easily circumvented by experienced attackers. Intrusion detection systems (IDSs) and vulnerability scanners may help system administrators to identify incidents or threats of individual attacks, but such systems are usually unaware of the relationships among attacks. An attacker can gradually elevate his/her privileges through multiple interdependent attacks on intermediate victims before finally reaching the attack goal. Such a cleverly crafted *multi-step* intrusion creates nightmares to system administrators because it is usually difficult to manually identify correlated attacks from the large volume of intrusion alerts.

A key obstacle to securing computer networks against potential attacks is the lack of an automated approach to generating feasible solutions for improving networks' security. To defend against multi-step intrusions, researchers have recently proposed techniques for correlating isolated vulnerabilities and weaknesses (next chapter will give a brief review of the literature). However, these techniques again leave the correlated results for humans to interpret, which in practice is usually a daunting task. Moreover, most techniques focus on detecting, analyzing and interpreting the risks, rather than providing direct solutions for securing networks against such threats. In particular, various analyses of *attack graphs* have been proposed to indicate possible sequences of vulnerabilities that attackers may exploit during a multi-step intrusion [1,4], but such an analysis does not directly provide a solution to stop the identified attacks. In fact, removing vulnerabilities will usually incur certain technical (e.g., replacing hardware or upgrading software) or administrative costs (e.g., loss in functionality or convenience), such that in practice simply removing all known vulnerabilities is usually not a viable option. It is usually a tedious and error-prone process for human analysts to identify and prioritize different vulnerabilities and weaknesses for patching or fixing. Therefore, a systematic approach to automatically generating feasible hardening solutions and ranking such solutions based on decreasing costs will make network hardening a science, rather than an art.

On the other hand, developing an automated approach, instead of solely relying on human analysts' knowledge and experiences, to improve network security has also become practically feasible due to latest research advances. First, most vulnerabilities can be discovered using existing vulnerability scanning tools (e.g., Nessus [2]). Second, technical details of such vulnerabilities (e.g., their prerequisites and consequences) are readily available from public databases (e.g., the National Vulnerability Database (NVD) [3]). Third, advances on topological vulnerability analysis using attack graphs [1, 4] have made it possible to understand how different vulnerabilities may be combined during actual attacks, and such increased understanding allows us to evaluate sequences of correlated vulnerabilities to judge their overall impact on a network's security. Armed with such tools and capabilities, we are now ready to answer a series of questions, which comprise our definition of *network hardening*, as follows:

- How can we find potential enforceable solutions for preventing multi-step intrusions targeting critical network assets?

- How can we enumerate all such solutions and rank them based on relative costs to select the most cost-effective ones?
- How can we handle hardening solutions with conflicting or overlapping actions that cannot be independently implemented?
- How can we achieve all these goals within a reasonable time constraint even for large networks?

1.2 Contribution

This book answers the four questions raised in the previous section. The following provides an overview of our main contribution.

- First, we discuss related work on network hardening and attack graphs. We also review necessary background information on relevant topics to make the book more self-contained.
- Second, we describe a solution to automate the task of hardening a network against multi-step intrusions. Unlike existing approaches whose solutions require removing exploits, our solution is comprised of initially satisfied conditions only. Our solution is thus more enforceable, because the initial conditions can be independently disabled, whereas exploits are usually consequences of other exploits and hence cannot be disabled without removing the causes. More specifically, we first represent given critical resources as a logic proposition of initial conditions. We then simplify the proposition to make hardening options explicit. Among the options we finally choose solutions with the minimum cost. We present a formal definition of the minimum network hardening problem using logic programming, and then describe an improved one-pass algorithm for deriving the logic proposition while avoiding logic loops.
- Third, we observe that the previous approach to network hardening looks for exact solutions and thus does not scale. Further, hardening elements have been treated independently, which is inappropriate for real environments. For example, the cost for patching many systems may be nearly the same as for patching a single one. Or patching a vulnerability may have the same effect as blocking traffic with a firewall, while blocking a port may deny legitimate service. By failing to account for such hardening interdependencies, the resulting recommendations can be unrealistic and far from optimal. Instead, we formalize the notion of hardening strategy in terms of allowable actions, and define a cost model that takes into account the impact of interdependent hardening actions. We also introduce a near-optimal approximation algorithm that scales linearly with the size of the graphs, which we validate experimentally.

The remainder of this book is organized as follows. Chapter 2 provides a literature review. Chapter 3 reviews the basic concepts of attack graphs and provides a motivating example to demonstrate the need for network hardening solutions. Chapter 4 presents an automated approach to minimum-cost network hardening in order to answer the first two questions raised at the end of Sect. 1.1. Chapter 5 then devises a heuristic solution to address the scalability issue and to handle dependent hardening options in order to answer the last two questions. Finally, Chap. 6 concludes the book and gives future directions.

References

1. P. Ammann, D. Wijesekera, and S. Kaushik.   Scalable, graph-based network vulnerability analysis. In *Proceedings of ACM CCS'02*, 2002.
2. R. Deraison. Nessus scanner, 1999. Available at http://www.nessus.org.
3. National vulnerability database. available at: http://www.nvd.org, May 9, 2008.
4. O. Sheyner, J. Haines, S. Jha, R. Lippmann, and J.M. Wing. Automated generation and analysis of attack graphs. In *Proceedings of the IEEE S&P'02*, 2002.

Chapter 2
Related Work

In this chapter, we provide a brief review of related work, including attack graphs and applications, existing network hardening techniques, and other relevant topics, such as alert correlation and security metrics.

2.1 Attack Graph

A number of tools are available for scanning network vulnerabilities, such as Nessus [12], Nmap [35], Snort [53], Cisco security scanner, System Scanner by ISS [21], CyberCop [7] and Computer Oracle and Password System (COPS) [14]. Those solutions are being applied in real world networks and they can help to identify weaknesses and flaws in such networks. However, most existing solutions usually identify vulnerabilities or attacks in isolation, which only provides a partial picture about securing a network since many attackers may employ sophisticated multi-step attacks to breach a seemingly well guarded network.

Attack graphs are constructed by analyzing the inter-dependency between vulnerabilities and security conditions that have been identified in the target network [2, 8, 14, 22, 40, 44, 51, 52, 56, 60, 73]. Such analysis can be either forward starting from the initial state [44, 60] or backward from the goal state [51, 56]. Model checking was first used to analyze whether the given goal state is reachable from the initial state [49, 51] but later used to enumerate all possible sequences of attacks between the two states [24, 56].

More specifically, Phillips and Swiler [44, 60] propose the concept of attack graph and they also present a graph-based approach for generating attack graphs. In their model, the inputs of an attack graph include configuration files, attacker profiles, and a database of attack templates, which must be manually created. The nodes of the attack graph are attack templates instantiated with particular users and machines, whereas edges are labeled with probabilities of success or cost of attacks.

L. Wang et al., *Network Hardening: An Automated Approach to Improving Network Security*, SpringerBriefs in Computer Science, DOI 10.1007/978-3-319-04612-9_2,
© The Author(s) 2014

The graphs can be analyzed to find the shortest paths between given start and end nodes. The idea of grouping similar nodes is mentioned although the correctness critically depends on identical configuration among such nodes.

Another model [61] expresses attack graphs with the require and provide approach using the precondition and postcondition of each exploit. For each successful attack, the attacker can obtain the ability to perform more attack steps so each successful exploitation increases his/her capabilities in launching new attacks. An attack specification language JIGSAW is used in describing attack steps. The language requires low level details of capabilities and requirements of attacks which may be hard to obtain. This require and provide approach brings flexibility in discovering potentially new attack scenarios. Using this language and the given specifications, an IDS and attack analysis system can be created.

In [51], model checking is applied to the analysis of multi-step network attacks. Known vulnerabilities on network hosts, connectivity between hosts, initial capabilities of the attacker are described as states and exploits as transitions between states. This model is given to a model checker as its input and the reachability in terms of given goal states is given as a query. The model checker then produces a counterexample if a sequence of exploits can lead to goal states. Such a sequence of exploits indicates a potential attack that must be avoided to secure the network. The term *topological vulnerability analysis* is coined in [52] which provides more details on how connectivity should be modeled at different layers.

In [24, 56], model checking is used for a different purpose, that is to enumerate all attack paths. A modified model checker is used to take as input the finite-state machine created from network information. The model checker provides all counterexamples to a query about the safety of the goal states. Those are essentially the possible attack paths. Other types of analysis are also discussed by the authors, including how to find a *cut set* in the attack graph, such that goal conditions can no longer be reached. The problem of finding the minimum possible attack that leads to the given goal conditions is shown to be intractable. One apparent limitation of this approach is that all attack paths are explicitly enumerated in its result, which leads to a combinatorial explosion.

A *monotonicity assumption* is adopted in [2] to address the scalability of model checking-based approaches. It states exploits will never cause the attacker to relinquish any previously obtained privileges. Attack paths can then be implicitly modeled as paths in a directed graph including exactly one copy of each exploit and its pre- and post-conditions; edges interconnect exploits to their conditions. The assumption thus reduces the complexity of attack graph from exponential to polynomial in the number of hosts. However, it also makes some attacks impossible if they disable services or invalidate vulnerabilities. Attack graphs are generated using a two-pass search that first links exploits by starting from the attacker's initial state and then removes those irrelevant states by searching backward from the goal state.

In [41] the authors proposed a logic-based approach to attack graph generation to improve the efficiency. Using this approach, the generated attack graph always has a polynomial size in the size of analyzed network. A Network security analyzer

MulVAL is used to build the attack graph generation tool. Here, each node of the attack graph represents a logical statement and the edges define the relationship between network configuration and what the privileges the attacker potentially could gain. Here, the main focus is on the root causes of the attack. Using this logical attack graph representation, one can obtain all the possible attack scenarios using a simple depth-first search. Using this representation, it can also be ensured that an attack graph will always have a polynomial size in the size of the network.

Attack graphs have been used for correlating intrusion alerts into attack scenarios [36, 67, 68]. Such alert correlation methods are parallel to our work, because they aim to employ the knowledge encoded in attack graphs for detecting and taking actions against actual intrusions, whereas our work aims to harden the network before any intrusion may happen. The relationship between those methods and our work is analogous to that between IDSs and vulnerability scanners, although IDSs and vulnerability scanners work on the alert and vulnerability level, whereas the alert correlation methods and our methods work at a higher level, i.e., the attack scenarios. In forensics, attack graph is also use to find probable attacks and to assess damages of the system [59]. For taking legal action against the attacker, the analyst needs to show attack steps as evidence. Using attack graph, the whole attack paths can be matched to data extracted from IDS logs.

2.2   Network Hardening

In [56] a *minimum critical set* is computed which is basically the minimum set of exploits in the attack graph by disabling which we can harden the network. The minimum critical attack set is essentially the concept of a cut set in graph theory. In [2], the authors propose an algorithm called findMinimul to find the attack that takes the least number of steps from the initial state to the goal condition to launch an attack. Another such approach proposed in [24] introduces the minimum critical attack set in a more scalable way. However, all these solutions cannot be directly used by system administrators as the set of exploits to be disabled are unavoidable consequences of other exploits, which must be disabled in the first place.

We introduce the concept of network hardening with respect to initially satisfied conditions in [37] and later refine it in [69]. In contrast to the above minimum critical set-based approaches, we argue that disabling initial conditions is a better choice with respect to the need of security administrators. To disable exploits in the critical set, we have to also disable the causes of such exploits, which ultimately leads to a set of security conditions that are initially satisfied and do not depend on others. Such initial conditions are only the pre-condition of some exploits but they are not the post condition of any exploit. This indicates that these conditions can be disabled independently. Therefore, an effective hardening measure is to find the set of initial conditions disabling which can disable the goal conditions. However, as we show in [1], this approach has an unavoidable exponential worst-case complexity, because the result itself may be exponential in size. So, for larger networks, enforcing this approach will be costly or even impossible depending on the number of hosts and their connectivity. Therefore, we address this issue with a heuristic approach that yields reasonably good results in significantly less time. In this book, we develop a more comprehensive and coherent study on network hardening based on those previous work.

2.3   Other Related Topics

Parallel to network hardening, alert correlation aims to understand multi-step attacks from the attack's point of view. It reconstructs multi-step attack scenarios from isolated alerts. This may employ prior knowledge about attack strategies [6, 10, 11, 13] or the causal relationships between attacks [5, 32, 33]. Those methods may either aggregate alerts with similar attributes [4, 9, 58, 63] or statistical patterns [25, 46]. Hybrid approaches also exist that combine different techniques for better results [33, 47, 71]. Alerts missed by IDSs can be tolerated by clustering alerts with similar attributes [34], and incomplete knowledge can be pieced together through statistical analyses [46, 47]. Alert correlation techniques are also used for other purposes such as to relate alerts to the same thread of attacks [20]. The privacy issue of alert correlation is investigated in [72]. Alert correlation is a potential method for dealing with insider attacks in [48, 50]. Existing efforts on integrating information from different sources exist, such as the model in *M2D2* [31] and the Bayesian network-based approach [74]. Some commercial products claim to support realtime analyses of alerts such as Tivoli Risk Manager [19].

An interesting future direction in network hardening is to integrate the network hardening techniques with various efforts on security metrics and security quantification. There exist numerous standardization efforts on security metrics, such as the Common Vulnerability Scoring System (CVSS) [30] and, more recently, the Common Weakness Scoring System (CWSS) [62]. The former focuses on ranking known vulnerabilities, whereas the latter on software weaknesses. Both CVSS and CWSS measure the relative severity of individual vulnerabilities in isolation and do not address their overall impact. On the other hand, these efforts form a practical foundation for research on security metrics, as they provide security analysts and vendors standard ways for assigning numerical scores to known vulnerabilities which are already available in public vulnerability databases, such as the National Vulnerability Database (NVD) [38]. On the research front, network security metrics has attracted much attention, as surveyed in [23, 54, 64]. In particular, the Network Compromise Percentage Metric (NCP) is proposed while evaluating the so-called *defense in depth* strategy using attack graphs [27], which basically indicates the percentage of network assets that may be compromised by attackers. In another work [29], the authors rank states in an attack graph based on probabilities of attackers reaching these states during a random simulation; the PageRank algorithm is adapted for such a ranking; a key assumption made in this work is that attackers would progress along different paths in an attack graph in a random fashion.

A similar work replaces attack trees with more advanced attack graphs and replace attack paths with attack scenarios [43]. A Mean Time-to-Compromise metric is proposed based on the predator state-space model (SSM) used in the biological sciences in [26]; defined as the average time required for compromising networks, the metric provides richer semantics than other abstract metrics; the main limitation of this work lies in an oversimplified model of network intrusions and differences between vulnerabilities. A recent work proposes a risk management framework using Bayesian networks to quantify the chances of attacks and to develop a security mitigation and management plan [45]. Another recent study of several CVSS-based vulnerability metrics shows the correlation between those metrics and the time to compromise of a system [17]. In our recent work, we have proposed a general framework for designing network security metrics [70], Bayesian network-based metrics [15], a probabilistic approach [65], a k-zero day safety metric [66], a base metric-level framework [3], and a mean time-to-compromise approach [39]. Parallel to our work on probabilistic security metrics, the authors in [18] address several important issues in calculating such metrics including the dependencies between different attack sequences in an attack graph and cyclic structures in such graphs.

Another interesting future direction in network hardening is to address the threat of *zero day attacks*. Most existing work focus on known vulnerabilities in a network. A few exceptions include an empirical study on the total number of zero day vulnerabilities available on a single day based on existing facts about vulnerabilities [28], a report on the popularity of zero day vulnerabilities among attackers [16], an empirical study on software vulnerabilities' life cycles [55], and more recently an effort on estimating the effort required for developing new exploits [57]. Finally, in the context of software security, the attack surface metric measures how likely a software is vulnerable to known or unknown attacks based on the degree of exposure [42].

References

1. Massimiliano Albanese, Sushil Jajodia, and Steven Noel. Time-efficient and cost-effective network hardening using attack graphs. In *Proceedings of the 42nd Annual IEEE/IFIP International Conference on Dependable Systems and Networks (DSN 2012)*, Boston, MA, USA, June 2012.
2. P. Ammann, D. Wijesekera, and S. Kaushik. Scalable, graph-based network vulnerability analysis. In *Proceedings of ACM CCS'02*, 2002.
3. Pengsu Cheng, Lingyu Wang, Sushil Jajodia, and Anoop Singhal. Aggregating cvss base scores for semantics-rich network security metrics. In *Proceedings of the 31st IEEE International Symposium on Reliable Distributed Systems (SRDS 2012)*, pages 31–40. IEEE Computer Society, 2012.
4. F. Cuppens. Managing alerts in a multi-intrusion detection environment. In *Proceedings of the 17th Annual Computer Security Applications Conference (ACSAC'01)*, 2001.
5. F. Cuppens and A. Miege. Alert correlation in a cooperative intrusion detection framework. In *Proceedings of the IEEE Symposium on Security and Privacy*, pages 187–200, 2002.

6. F. Cuppens and R. Ortalo. LAMBDA: A language to model a database for detection of attacks. In *Proceedings of the 3rd International Symposium on Recent Advances in Intrusion Detection (RAID'01)*, pages 197–216, 2001.

7. Network associates,cybercop scanner. Available at http://www.nss.co.uk/grouptests/va/edition2/nai_cybercop_scanner/nai_cybercop_scanner.htm.

8. M. Dacier. Towards quantitative evaluation of computer security. Ph.D. Thesis, Institut National Polytechnique de Toulouse, 1994.

9. O. Dain and R.K. Cunningham. Building scenarios from a heterogeneous alert system. In *Proceedings of the 2001 IEEE Workshop on Information Assurance and Security*, 2001.

10. O. Dain and R.K. Cunningham. Fusing a heterogeneous alert stream into scenarios. In *Proceedings of the ACM Workshop on Data Mining for Security Applications*, pages 1–13, 2001.

11. H. Debar and A. Wespi. Aggregation and correlation of intrusion-detection alerts. In *Proceedings of the 3rd International Symposium on Recent Advances in Intrusion Detection (RAID'01)*, pages 85–103, 2001.

12. R. Deraison. Nessus scanner, 1999. Available at http://www.nessus.org.

13. S.T. Eckmann, G. Vigna, and R.A. Kemmerer. STATL: An attack language for state-based intrusion detection. *Journal of Computer Security*, 10(1/2):71–104, 2002.

14. D. Farmer and E.H. Spafford. The COPS security checker system. In *USENIX Summer*, pages 165–170, 1990.

15. M. Frigault, L. Wang, A. Singhal, and S. Jajodia. Measuring network security using dynamic bayesian network. In *Proceedings of 4th ACM QoP*, 2008.

16. A. Greenberg. Shopping for zero-days: A price list for hackers' secret software exploits. *Forbes*, 23 March 2012.

17. Hannes Holm, Mathias Ekstedt, and Dennis Andersson. Empirical analysis of system-level vulnerability metrics through actual attacks. *IEEE Trans. Dependable Secur. Comput.*, 9(6):825–837, November 2012.

18. J. Homer, X. Ou, and D. Schmidt. A sound and practical approach to quantifying security risk in enterprise networks. Technical Report, 2009.

19. IBM. IBM tivoli risk manager. Available at http://www.ibm.com/software/tivoli/products/risk-mgr/.

20. SRI International. Event monitoring enabling responses to anomalous live disturbances (EMERALD). Available at http://www.sdl.sri.com/projects/emerald/.

21. System Scanner Internet Security Systems. Internet security systems, system scanner. Available at http://www.iss.net.

22. S. Jajodia, S. Noel, and B. O'Berry. Topological analysis of network attack vulnerability. In V. Kumar, J. Srivastava, and A. Lazarevic, editors, *Managing Cyber Threats: Issues, Approaches and Challenges*. Kluwer Academic Publisher, 2003.

23. A. Jaquith. *Security Merics: Replacing Fear Uncertainty and Doubt*. Addison Wesley, 2007.

24. S. Jha, O. Sheyner, and J.M. Wing. Two formal analysis of attack graph. In *Proceedings of the 15th Computer Security Foundation Workshop (CSFW'02)*, 2002.

25. Klaus Julisch and Marc Dacier. Mining intrusion detection alarms for actionable knowledge. In *Proceedings of the eighth ACM SIGKDD international conference on Knowledge discovery and data mining*, pages 366–375, 2002.

26. D.J. Leversage and E.J. Byres. Estimating a system's mean time-to-compromise. *IEEE Security and Privacy*, 6(1):52–60, 2008.

27. R. Lippmann, K. Ingols, C. Scott, K. Piwowarski, K. Kratkiewicz, M. Artz, and R. Cunningham. Validating and restoring defense in depth using attack graphs. In *Proceedings of the 2006 IEEE conference on Military communications*, MILCOM'06, pages 981–990, Piscataway, NJ, USA, 2006. IEEE Press.

28. M.A. McQueen, T.A. McQueen, W.F. Boyer, and M.R. Chaffin. Empirical estimates and observations of 0day vulnerabilities. *Hawaii International Conference on System Sciences*, 0:1–12, 2009.

29. V. Mehta, C. Bartzis, H. Zhu, E.M. Clarke, and J.M. Wing. Ranking attack graphs. In *Recent Advances in Intrusion Detection 2006*, 2006.
30. P. Mell, K. Scarfone, and S. Romanosky. Common vulnerability scoring system. *IEEE Security & Privacy*, 4(6):85–89, 2006.
31. B. Morin, L. Mé, H. Debar, and M. Ducassé. M2D2: A formal data model for IDS alert correlation. In *Proceedings of the 5th International Symposium on Recent Advances in Intrusion Detection (RAID'02)*, pages 115–137, 2002.
32. P. Ning, Y. Cui, and D.S. Reeves. Constructing attack scenarios through correlation of intrusion alerts. In *Proceedings of the 9th ACM Conference on Computer and Communications Security (CCS'02)*, pages 245–254, 2002.
33. P. Ning and D. Xu. Learning attack strategies from intrusion alerts. In *Proceedings of the 10th ACM Conference on Computer and Communications Security (CCS'03)*, 2003.
34. P. Ning, D. Xu, C.G. Healey, and R.S. Amant. Building attack scenarios through integration of complementary alert correlation methods. In *Proceedings of the 11th Annual Network and Distributed System Security Symposium (NDSS'04)*, pages 97–111, 2004.
35. Nmap-network mapper. Available at http://nmap.org/index.html.
36. S. Noel and S. Jajodia. Correlating intrusion events and building attack scenarios through attack graph distance. In *Proceedings of the 20th Annual Computer Security Applications Conference (ACSAC'04)*, 2004.
37. S. Noel, S. Jajodia, B. O'Berry, and M. Jacobs. Efficient minimum-cost network hardening via exploit dependency grpahs. In *Proceedings of the 19th Annual Computer Security Applications Conference (ACSAC'03)*, 2003.
38. National vulnerability database. available at: http://www.nvd.org, May 9, 2008.
39. W. Nzoukou, L. Wang, S. Jajodia1, and A. Singhal. A unified framework for measuring a network's mean time-to-compromise. In *Proceedings of the 32nd IEEE International Symposium on Reliable Distributed Systems (SRDS 2013)*, pages 215–224, 2013.
40. R. Ortalo, Y. Deswarte, and M. Kaaniche. Experimenting with quantitative evaluation tools for monitoring operational security. *IEEE Trans. Software Eng.*, 25(5):633–650, 1999.
41. X. Ou, W.F. Boyer, and M.A. McQueen. A scalable approach to attack graph generation. In *Proceedings of the 13th ACM conference on Computer and communications security*, CCS'06, pages 336–345, New York, NY, USA, 2006. ACM.
42. J. Wing P. Manadhata. An attack surface metric. Technical Report CMU-CS-05-155, 2005.
43. J. Pamula, S. Jajodia, P. Ammann, and V. Swarup. A weakest-adversary security metric for network configuration security analysis. In *Proceedings of the ACM QoP*, pages 31–38, 2006.
44. C. Phillips and L. Swiler. A graph-based system for network-vulnerability analysis. In *Proceedings of the New Security Paradigms Workshop (NSPW'98)*, 1998.
45. Nayot Poolsappasit, Rinku Dewri, and Indrajit Ray. Dynamic security risk management using bayesian attack graphs. *IEEE Trans. Dependable Secur. Comput.*, 9(1):61–74, January 2012.
46. X. Qin and W. Lee. Statistical causality analysis of INFOSEC alert data. In *Proceedings of the 6th International Symposium on Recent Advances in Intrusion Detection (RAID 2003)*, pages 591–627, 2003.
47. X. Qin and W. Lee. Discovering novel attack strategies from INFOSEC alerts. In *Proceedings of the 9th European Symposium on Research in Computer Security (ESORICS 2004)*, pages 439–456, 2004.
48. A. R. Chinchani andIyer, H. Ngo, and S. Upadhyay. Towards a theory of insider threat assessment. In *Proceedings of the IEEE International Conference on Dependable Systems and Networks (DSN'05)*, 2005.
49. C.R. Ramakrishnan and R. Sekar. Model-based analysis of configuration vulnerabilities. *Journal of Computer Security*, 10(1/2):189–209, 2002.
50. I. Ray and N. Poolsappasit. Using attack trees to identify malicious attacks from authorized insiders. In *Proceedings of the 10th European Symposium on Research in Computer Security (ESORICS'05)*, 2005.

51. R. Ritchey and P. Ammann.   Using model checking to analyze network vulnerabilities. In *Proceedings of the 2000 IEEE Symposium on Security and Privacy*, pages 156–165, 2000.
52. R. Ritchey, B. O'Berry, and S. Noel. Representing TCP/IP connectivity for topological analysis of network security.   In *Proceedings of the 18th Annual Computer Security Applications Conference (ACSAC'02)*, page 25, 2002.
53. M. Roesch. Snort - lightweight intrusion detection for networks. In *Proceedings of the 1999 USENIX LISA Conference*, pages 229–238, 1999.
54. R.M. Savola. Towards a taxonomy for information security metrics. In *Proceedings of the 3rd ACM QoP*, pages 28–30. ACM, 2007.
55. M. Shahzad, M.Z. Shafiq, and A.X. Liu.   A large scale exploratory analysis of software vulnerability life cycles.   In *Proceedings of the 34th International Conference on Software Engineering (ICSE)*, 2012.
56. O. Sheyner, J. Haines, S. Jha, R. Lippmann, and J.M. Wing. Automated generation and analysis of attack graphs. In *Proceedings of the IEEE S&P'02*, 2002.
57. Teodor Sommestad, Hannes Holm, and Mathias Ekstedt.   Effort estimates for vulnerability discovery projects.   In *Proceedings of the 2012 45th Hawaii International Conference on System Sciences*, HICSS '12, pages 5564–5573, Washington, DC, USA, 2012. IEEE Computer Society.
58. S. Staniford, J.A. Hoagland, and J.M. McAlerney.   Practical automated detection of stealthy portscans. *Journal of Computer Security*, 10(1/2):105–136, 2002.
59. P. Stephenson. Using formal methods for forensic analysis of intrusion events- - a preliminary examination. white paper. available at http://www.imfgroup.com/DocumentLibrary.html.
60. L. Swiler, C. Phillips, D. Ellis, and S. Chakerian.   Computer attack graph generation tool.   In *Proceedings of the DARPA Information Survivability Conference & Exposition II (DISCEX'01)*, 2001.
61. S. Templeton and K. Levitt. A requires/provides model for computer attacks. In *Proceedings of the 2000 New Security Paradigms Workshop (NSPW'00)*, pages 31–38, 2000.
62. The MITRE Corporation.   Common weakness scoring system.   http://cwe.mitre.org/cwss/, 2010.
63. A. Valdes and K. Skinner.   Probabilistic alert correlation.   In *Proceedings of the 4th International Symposium on Recent Advances in Intrusion Detection*, pages 54–68, 2001.
64. V. Verendel.   Quantified security is a weak hypothesis: a critical survey of results and assumptions. In *Proceedings of the 2009 NSPW*, pages 37–50. ACM, 2009.
65. L. Wang, T. Islam, T. Long, A. Singhal, and S. Jajodia. An attack graph-based probabilistic security metric. In *Proceedings of the 22nd IFIP DBSec*, 2008.
66. L. Wang, S. Jajodia, A. Singhal, and S. Noel. k-zero day safety: Measuring the security risk of networks against unknown attacks. In *Proceedings of the 15th ESORICS*, pages 573–587, 2010.
67. L. Wang, A. Liu, and S. Jajodia. An efficient and unified approach to correlating, hypothesizing, and predicting intrusion alerts. In *Proceedings of the 10th European Symposium on Research in Computer Security (ESORICS 2005)*, pages 247–266, 2005.
68. L. Wang, A. Liu, and S. Jajodia.   Using attack graphs for correlating, hypothesizing, and predicting intrusion alerts. *Computer Communications*, 29(15):2917–2933, 2006.
69. L. Wang, S. Noel, and S. Jajodia.   Minimum-cost network hardening using attack graphs. *Computer Communications*, 29(18):3812–3824, 11 2006.
70. L. Wang, A. Singhal, and S. Jajodia.   Measuring network security using attack graphs. In *Proceedings of the 3rd ACM QoP*, New York, NY, USA, 2007. ACM Press.
71. D. Xu and P. Ning.   Alert correlation through triggering events and common resources. In *Proceedings of the 20th Annual Computer Security Applications Conference (ACSAC'04)*, pages 360–369, 2004.
72. D. Xu and P. Ning. Privacy-preserving alert correlation: A concept hierarchy based approach. In *Proceedings of the 21st Annual Computer Security Applications Conference (ACSAC'05)*, 2005.

73. D. Zerkle and K. Levitt. Netkuang - a multi-host configuration vulnerability checker. In *Proceedings of the 6th USENIX Unix Security Symposium (USENIX'96)*, 1996.
74. Y. Zhai, P. Ning, P. Iyer, and D. Reeves. Reasoning about complementary intrusion evidence. In *Proceedings of the 20th Annual Computer Security Applications Conference (ACSAC'04)*, pages 39–48, 2004.

Chapter 3
Attack Graph and Network Hardening

In this chapter, we briefly review some important concepts that are relevant to further discussions. First, we introduce attack graph and its related concepts. Second, we formalize the network hardening problem. Third, we briefly review standard heuristic approaches and their applicability to network hardening.

3.1 Attack Graph

Attack graphs represent prior knowledge about vulnerabilities, their dependencies, and network connectivity. There are two different representations possible for an attack graph. First, an attack graph can explicitly enumerate all possible sequences of vulnerabilities an attacker can follow, i.e., all possible *attack paths* [7, 10]. However, such graphs face a combinatorial explosion in the number of attack paths. Second, with a monotonicity assumption stating an attacker never relinquishes an obtained capability, an attack graph can record the dependency relationships among vulnerabilities and keep attack paths implicitly without losing any information [1]. The resulting attack graph has no duplicate vertices and hence has a polynomial size in the number of vulnerabilities multiplied by the number of connected pairs of hosts. We shall assume this latter notion of attack graphs.

Although attack graph can take various forms, we represent an attack graph as a directed graph with two type of vertices, *exploits* and *security conditions* (or simply *conditions* when no confusion is possible). Most generally, we denote an exploit as a predicate $v(h_s, h_m, h_d)$. This indicates an exploitation of the vulnerability v on the destination host h_d, initiated from the source host h_s, through an intermediate host h_m. Similarly, we write $v(h_s, h_d)$ or $v(h)$, respectively, for exploits involving two hosts (no intermediate host) or one (local) host.

A security condition is a predicate $c(h_s, h_d)$ that indicates a satisfied security-related condition c involving the source host h_s and the destination host h_d

L. Wang et al., *Network Hardening: An Automated Approach to Improving Network Security*, SpringerBriefs in Computer Science, DOI 10.1007/978-3-319-04612-9__3,

(when a condition involves a single host, we simply write $c(h)$). Examples of security conditions include the existence of a vulnerability or the connectivity between two hosts.

There are two types of directed edges that inter-connect exploits with conditions (but no edges directly between exploits or directly between conditions). First, an edge can point from a condition to an exploit. Such an edge denotes the *require* relation, which means the exploit cannot be executed unless the condition is satisfied. Second, an edge pointing from an exploit to a condition denotes the *imply* relation, which means executing the exploit will satisfy the condition. For example, an exploit usually requires the existence of the vulnerability on the destination host and the connectivity between the two hosts. We formally characterize attack graphs in Definition 3.1.

Definition 3.1. Given a set of exploits E, a set of conditions C, a *require* relation $R_r \subseteq C \times E$, and an *imply* relation $R_i \subseteq E \times C$, an *attack graph* G is the directed graph $G(E \cup C, R_r \cup R_i)$ ($E \cup C$ is the vertex set and $R_r \cup R_i$ the edge set).

One important aspect of attack graphs is that the require relation is always conjunctive, whereas the imply relation is always disjunctive. More specifically, an exploit cannot be realized until *all* of its required conditions have been satisfied, whereas a condition is satisfied if *any* of the realized exploits implies the condition. Exceptions to the above requirements do exist. First, an exploit with multiple variations may require different sets of conditions, whence the require relation for this exploit is disjunctive (between these sets of conditions). This case can be handled by having a separate vertex for each variation of the exploit such that the require relation for each variation is still strictly conjunctive.

On the other hand, a collection of exploits may jointly imply a condition whereas none of them alone can do so, whence the imply relation becomes conjunctive for this condition. This case can be handled by inserting dummy conditions and exploits to capture the conjunctive relationship. For example, suppose both e_1 and e_2 are required to make a condition c satisfied. We insert two dummy conditions c_1 and c_2 and a dummy exploit e_3 into the attack graph. The edges are inserted such that e_1 and e_2 imply c_1 and c_2, respectively, and c_1 and c_2 are required by e_3, which in turn implies c. Now the conjunctive relationship that both e_1 and e_2 are required for c to be satisfied is encoded in the fact that e_3 requires both c_1 and c_2. As will be discussed later, the result of our methods includes only those conditions that are not implied by any exploit, and hence introducing dummy conditions and exploits does not affect the effectiveness of our methods.

Figure 3.1 shows a small example of attack graph in which exploits appear as rectangles and conditions as ovals; purple ovals represent initial conditions, whereas blue ovals represent intermediate conditions. We assume a simple scenario where a file server (host 1) offers the File Transfer Protocol (ftp), secure shell (ssh), and remote shell (rsh) services; a database server (host 2) offers ftp and rsh services. The firewall only allows ftp, ssh, and rsh traffic from a user workstation (host 0) to both servers. The attack graph represents three self-explanatory sequences of attacks (attack paths).

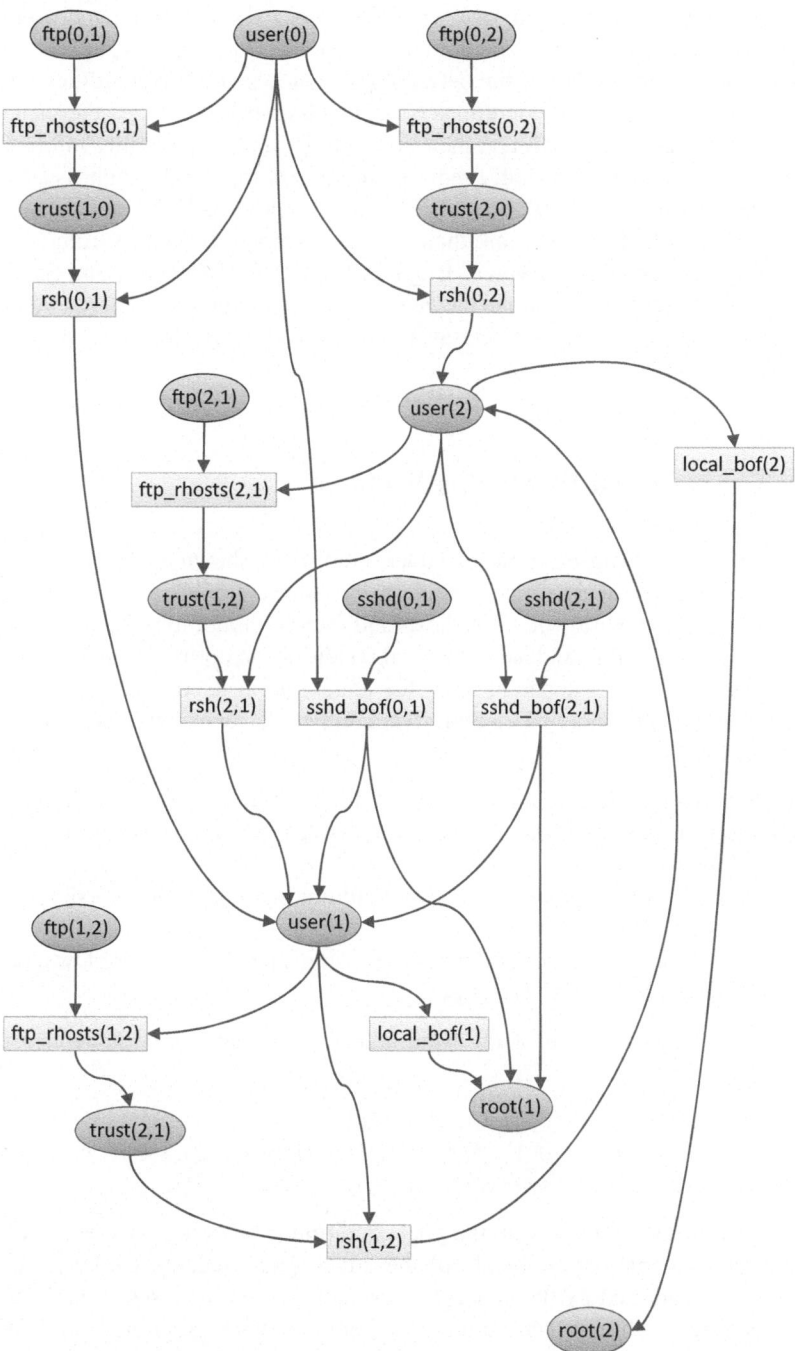

Fig. 3.1 An example of attack graph, including initial conditions (*purple ovals*), exploits (*green rectangles*), and intermediate conditions (*blue ovals*) (Color figure online)

To generate an attack graph, two types of inputs are necessary, namely, *domain knowledge* and *network map*. The domain knowledge represents expert knowledge about the dependency relationship between different type of vulnerabilities, such as the pre-conditions and post-conditions of each vulnerability. On the other hand, the network map represents hosts and their connectivity and vulnerability information. We assume the domain knowledge required for generating attack graphs is available from databases like NVD [9], or tools like the Topological Vulnerability Analysis (TVA) system, which covers more than 37,000 vulnerabilities taken from 24 information sources including X-Force, Bugtraq, CVE, CERT, Nessus, and Snort [6]. On the other hand, we assume the network map including vulnerabilities and connectivity can be obtained using available network scanning tools, such as the Nessus scanner [3].

3.2   The Network Hardening Problem

We revisit our running example of attack graphs, as shown in Fig. 3.1, in order to motivate further discussions. Although the attack graph in Fig. 3.1 depicts a relatively simple scenario with three hosts and four vulnerabilities, because multiple interleaved attack paths can lead to the goal condition, an optimal solution to harden the network is still not apparent from the attack graph itself, and finding such a solution by hand may not be straightforward, either. As an example of attack paths, the attacker can

- first establish a trust relationship from his machine (host 0) to host 2 (the condition $trust(2,0)$) via the ftp rhosts vulnerability on host 2 (the exploit $ftp\_rhosts(0,2)$),
- then gain user privilege on host 2 (the condition $user(2)$) with an rsh login (the exploit $rsh(0,2)$), and
- finally achieve the goal condition $root(2)$ using a local buffer overflow attack on host 2 (the exploit $local\_bof(2)$).

The following are some of the valid attack paths that can be generated using existing algorithms [1].

- $ftp\_rhosts(0,2), rsh(0,2), local\_bof(2)$
- $ftp\_rhosts(0,1), rsh(0,1), ftp\_rhosts(1,2), rsh(1,2), local\_bof(2)$
- $sshd\_bof(0,2), ftp\_rhosts(1,2), rsh(1,2), local\_bof(2)$

Roughly speaking, to prevent the goal condition from being satisfied, a solution to network hardening must break all the attack paths leading to the goal. This intuition was captured by the concept of *critical set*, that is, a set of exploits (and corresponding conditions) whose removal from the attack graph will invalidate all attack paths [7, 10]. It has also been shown that finding critical sets with the minimum cardinality is NP-hard, whereas finding a minimal critical set (that is, a critical set with no proper subset being a critical set) is polynomial. Based on the above attack paths, there are many minimal critical sets, such as $\{rsh(0,2), rsh(1,2)\}$, $\{ftp\_rhosts(0,2), rsh(1,2)\}$, $\{ftp\_rhosts(1,2), rsh(0,2)\}$, and so on. If any of those sets of exploits could be completely removed, all the attack paths would become invalid, and hence the goal condition is safe.

However, the above solution ignores the following important fact. Not all exploits are under the direct control of administrators. An exploit can only be removed by disabling its required conditions, but not all conditions can be disabled at will. Intuitively, a consequence cannot be removed without removing its causes. Some conditions are implied by other exploits. Such *intermediate* conditions cannot be independently disabled without removing those exploits that imply them. Only those *initial* conditions that are not implied by any exploit can be disabled independently of other exploits or conditions. Hence, it is important to distinguish between those two kinds of conditions, as formally stated in Definition 3.2.

Definition 3.2. In an attack graph $G(E \cup C, R_r \cup R_i)$, initial conditions refer to the subset of conditions $C_i = \{c \mid$ there does not exist $e \in E$ such that $(e,c) \in R_i\}$, whereas intermediate conditions (or simply conditions if no ambiguity is possible) refer to the subset $C - C_i$.

In the previous example, each of the rsh exploits requires intermediate conditions only, and hence cannot be removed without first removing other exploits. For example, the exploit $rsh(1,2)$ cannot be independently removed, because the two conditions it requires, $trust(2,1)$ and $user(1)$, are both intermediate conditions and cannot be independently disabled. As long as an attacker can satisfy those two conditions through other exploits (for example, $ftp\_rhosts(1,2)$ and $sshd\_bof(2,1)$), the realization of the exploit $rsh(1,2)$ is unavoidable. In practice, although one can stop the rsh service on host 2 to remove this exploit, this action adversely reduces the availability of services to normal users. Hence, any of the above minimal critical sets, such as $\{rsh(0,2), rsh(1,2)\}$, is theoretically a sound solution, but practically not enforceable.

The above discussions show that a network-hardening solution based on exploits or intermediate conditions cannot be easily enforced. This observation motivates us to pose the following question: *Which of the initial conditions must be disabled, if the goal conditions are never to be satisfied?* Our solution will thus be actually possible to implement, because it only includes initial conditions, which can be independently disabled. To more formally state the above problem, it is convenient to interpret an attack graph as a simple logic program as follows. Each exploit or condition in the attack graph is interpreted as a logic variable. The interdependency between exploits and conditions now becomes logic propositions involving the two connectives AND and OR, with AND between the conditions required by each exploit and OR between the exploits implying each condition.

Because of the interpretation of attack graphs as a logic program, all the variables are Boolean. A true initial condition means the condition is satisfied and a false one means it has been disabled for hardening the network. A true exploit means it has been realized because all of its required conditions are satisfied. A true intermediate condition means it has been satisfied by at least one realized exploit implying the condition. With this logic program, the *network hardening* problem is simply to find the value assignments to the initial conditions such that a given set of goal conditions are all false. Those are more formally stated in Definition 3.3 and illustrated in Example 3.1.

Definition 3.3. Given an attack graph $G(E \cup C, R_r \cup R_i)$ with a given set of goal conditions $C_g \subseteq C$, let $P(G)$ denote a logic program comprised of the following clauses.

- $e \leftarrow c_1 \wedge c_2 \wedge \cdots c_n$, where $e \in E$ and each c_i is in $R_r(e)$
- $c \leftarrow e_1 \vee e_2 \vee \cdots e_m$, where $c \in C$ and each e_i is in $R_i(c)$ (note the disjunctions will need to be separated into different clauses)

The *network hardening* problem is to satisfy the goal $\neg c_1 \wedge \neg c_2 \wedge \cdots \neg c_l$ where each c_i is in C_g.

Example 3.1. For the attack graph G shown in Fig. 3.1, the following are examples of the clauses in $P(G)$

- $ftp\_rhosts(0, 1) \leftarrow ftp(0, 1) \wedge user(0)$
- $rsh(0, 1) \leftarrow trust(1, 0) \wedge user(0)$
- $user(1) \leftarrow rsh(0, 1)$
- $user(1) \leftarrow rsh(2, 1)$
- $user(1) \leftarrow sshd\_bof(0, 1)$
- $user(1) \leftarrow sshd\_bof(2, 1)$
- $root(2) \leftarrow local\_bof(2)$

To harden the network, we need only to find a value assignment to the initial conditions such that the goal clause $\neg root(2)$ is satisfied.

We can easily derive a logic proposition that represents the goal clause in terms of initial conditions. This proposition is thus the necessary and sufficient condition for hardening the network such that none of the goal conditions can be satisfied. However, such a proposition usually implies multiple non-comparable options. Moreover, such options are not always so apparent from the proposition itself. Therefore, we first convert the proposition to its disjunctive normal form (DNF). Each disjunction in the DNF thus represents a particular sufficient option in hardening the network. Given the cost for disabling each initial condition, we can then choose the minimum-cost solution among those options in the DNF.

As in previous work [8], we assume the cost of disabling each initial condition in attack graphs is already given as a numerical value. In practice, the assignment of such costs will depend on specific applications' needs. For example, the cost of upgrading hardware or software may be measured in dollars, and administrative costs may be measured in terms of time. How to practically assign meaningful costs is beyond the scope of this book.

3.3   Standard Heuristic Approaches

In order to solve large-sized combinatorial search problems in reasonable time, there already exist many different heuristic methods such as simulated annealing, genetic algorithm, Tabu search, GRAPS, Harmony Search, A^*, honey bee algorithm, and so on, which provide general means to search for good, but not always optimal, solutions [2, 5]. We briefly review some of the common heuristic algorithms in the following.

- **Simulated Annealing (SA)**
  Simulated Annealing is based on an analogy between combinatorial optimization and the annealing process of solids. It is for finding a good solution to an optimization problem by trying random variations of the current solution. This technique relies on the idea of thermal annealing which aims to obtain perfect crystallization by a slow enough temperature reduction by allowing a certain time for the atoms to attain the lowest energy state. SA always accepts a move from current state to a neighbor state but also accepts an uphill move with a given probability. And this probability depends on the difference between the function value and T (temperature), which is gradually decreased during the process. A given number is used for as a stopping criterion, which is the number of iterations [4].
- **Tabu Search**
  This search is designed to explore discrete search spaces where the set of neighbors is finite. This method avoids cycling, which means visiting the same solution more than once, by using a short-term memory known as the Tabu list. This list contains the solutions which are most recently visited. The stopping criterion is defined in terms of improvement over the current solution [4].
- **Genetic algorithm (GA)**
  This is a population-based method that works simultaneously on the whole set of solutions, namely, the population. This technique imitates the evolutionary process of species. Here the new candidate solutions are selected with the crossover by combining part of the parents with some random mutations. After that the child nodes that have good characteristics from parents are given higher probability to survive or chosen as tentative solutions. Initially, it accepts a set of solutions and then constructs sets of neighboring solutions. It then examines the crossover to increase the population and select the better solutions. A given number is regarded as the stopping criterion [4].
- **Ant colonies (AC)**
  Here the way of search is similar to the way that ants look for foods and how they find their way back to a nest. One ant explores the neighborhood randomly and when it finds some food it will start to transport that to the nest leaving traces for the other ants to the source. So, more ants can find the food by traveling a shorter distance on the same trail. Then, they look for more food by repeating the same procedure. The search area of the ant is a discrete set from which the elements are selected and the food is the function that can provide some objective for the solution, and the trail is implemented as an adaptive memory [4].

The above techniques mostly focus on optimally exploring the search space such that the heuristic result will be closer to the optimal result. In this book, instead of simply applying these standard techniques, we study heuristics that focus on exploring certain unique properties of attack graphs, such as the disjunctive and conjunctive relationships among exploits and conditions, in order to improve the quality of the heuristic results. As to exploring the search space (that is, the power set of all initial conditions), we only employ a simple method. Therefore, the above standard heuristic methods are in parallel to, and can potentially be integrated into, our solution to optimize the way it explores the search space, which we regard as our future work.

References

1. P. Ammann, D. Wijesekera, and S. Kaushik. Scalable, graph-based network vulnerability analysis. In *Proceedings of ACM CCS'02*, 2002.
2. Christian Blum and Andrea Roli. Metàheuristics in combinatorial optimization: Overview and conceptual comparison. *ACM Comput. Surv.*, 35(3):268–308, 2003.
3. R. Deraison. Nessus scanner, 1999. Available at http://www.nessus.org.
4. Manfred GILLI and Peter WINKER. A review of heuristic optimization methods in econometrics. Swiss Finance Institute Research Paper Series 08–12, Swiss Finance Institute, 2008.
5. G. Laporte I.H. Osman. Metaheuristics: A bibliography. *Annals of Operations Research*, 63(5):511–623, 1996.
6. S. Jajodia, S. Noel, and B. O'Berry. Topological analysis of network attack vulnerability. In V. Kumar, J. Srivastava, and A. Lazarevic, editors, *Managing Cyber Threats: Issues, Approaches and Challenges*. Kluwer Academic Publisher, 2003.
7. S. Jha, O. Sheyner, and J.M. Wing. Two formal analysis of attack graph. In *Proceedings of the 15th Computer Security Foundation Workshop (CSFW'02)*, 2002.
8. S. Noel, S. Jajodia, B. O'Berry, and M. Jacobs. Efficient minimum-cost network hardening via exploit dependency grpahs. In *Proceedings of the 19th Annual Computer Security Applications Conference (ACSAC'03)*, 2003.
9. National vulnerability database. available at: http://www.nvd.org, May 9, 2008.
10. O. Sheyner, J. Haines, S. Jha, R. Lippmann, and J.M. Wing. Automated generation and analysis of attack graphs. In *Proceedings of the IEEE S&P'02*, 2002.

Chapter 4
Minimum-Cost Network Hardening

Abstract In defending one's network against cyber attacks, certain vulnerabilities may seem acceptable risks when considered in isolation. But an intruder can often infiltrate a seemingly well-guarded network through a multi-step intrusion, in which each step prepares for the next. Attack graphs can reveal the threat by enumerating possible sequences of exploits that can be followed to compromise given critical resources. However, attack graphs do not directly provide a solution to remove the threat. Finding a solution by hand is error-prone and tedious, particularly for larger and less secure networks whose attack graphs are overly complicated. In this chapter, we propose a solution to automate the task of hardening a network against multi-step intrusions. More specifically, we first represent given critical resources as a logic proposition of initial conditions. We then simplify the proposition to make hardening options explicit. Among the options we finally choose solutions with the minimum cost.

4.1 Overview

As we have mentioned in Chap. 1, attackers typically employ multiple attacks to evade security measures and to gradually gain privileges and approach the final goal. Such a multi-step network intrusion can often infiltrate even a seemingly well guarded network. Isolated vulnerabilities reported by vulnerability scanners (e.g., Nessus [2]) may not seem to be a serious threat until they are cleverly combined by attackers. The completeness of a penetration testing usually heavily depends on techniques of the red team, and is prone to human errors.

As mentioned in Chap. 2, existing approaches build *attack graphs* to represent attack paths, i.e., the possible sequences of vulnerabilities that attackers may exploit during a multi-step intrusion. However, while attack graphs reveal the threats, they do not directly provide a solution to harden the network against them. Removing vulnerabilities usually incurs different costs, and in practice it is usually infeasible to remove all identified vulnerabilities. A critical but unanswered question in

L. Wang et al., *Network Hardening: An Automated Approach to Improving Network Security*, SpringerBriefs in Computer Science, DOI 10.1007/978-3-319-04612-9__4,
© The Author(s) 2014

defending against multi-step intrusions is thus: *Which of the vulnerabilities should be removed, such that none of the attack paths leading to given critical resources can be realized, where such removal incurs the least cost?* Finding an answer to this question manually is error-prone and tedious, and becomes infeasible for larger and less secure networks whose attack graphs are too complicated.

As also reviewed in Chap. 3, one previous effort aims to compute a minimal set of vulnerabilities as the solution to harden the network [3,6]. However, such a solution is not directly enforceable, because some of the vulnerabilities are consequences of exploiting other vulnerabilities, and the consequences cannot be removed without first removing the causes. For example, the solution may require an FTP-related vulnerability to be removed. The vulnerability depends on the existence of the vulnerable FTP service on the destination host and the FTP access privilege for source hosts, and the latter may further depend on other vulnerabilities on the source hosts. Clearly, there are multiple choices with different costs in removing this single vulnerability. This shows that a minimal set of vulnerabilities is not necessarily a minimal solution, considering the vulnerabilities they may implicitly depend on.

The method introduced in this chapter takes into account the dependency relationships among vulnerabilities in deriving hardening solutions. As described in Chap. 3, we view each vulnerability as a Boolean variable, and we derive a logic proposition to represent the negation of given critical resources in terms of initially satisfied security-related conditions (or initial conditions for short). This proposition is thus the necessary and sufficient condition for protecting the critical resources. To make hardening options explicit, we transform this logic proposition into its disjunctive normal form (DNF). Each disjunction in the DNF provides a different option in hardening the network. We then choose options with the minimum costs based on given assumptions on the cost of initial conditions.

Our solution removes the previously mentioned limitation of existing approaches, because the hardening options require disabling initial conditions only. Each initial condition can be independently disabled because they do not depend on other vulnerabilities or conditions. For example, instead of requiring the removal of an FTP vulnerability, our solution may require disabling the vulnerable FTP service or denying FTP accesses to certain hosts, which are both readily enforceable. In the simplification of the logic proposition, we can identify seemingly relevant initial conditions whose removal does not really help to protect the critical resources. Such insights are important in keeping the cost of network hardening minimal, but they are also impossible to obtain in previous approaches.

Besides the above main contribution, another contribution of the current chapter is as follows. Instead of depending on an extra forward search to remove cycles in attack graphs, we propose a different algorithm that searches the attack graph and removes cycles all in one-pass. This approach removes the difficulty of the previous method in dealing with cycles that cannot be easily removed in the forward search. As a side benefit, it also improves the performance by avoiding the preprocessing step of a forward search.

The rest of this chapter is organized as follows. Section 4.2 derives a network hardening solution based on graph searching. Section 4.3 discusses how to choose optimal solutions based on the cost. Section 4.4 provides a case study to illustrate the proposed method. Finally, Sect. 4.5 concludes the chapter.

4.2   Graph Search-Based Network Hardening Algorithm

By Definition 3.3, we can certainly depend on logic programming techniques to find a solution to the problem. However, considering the simplicity of the logic program, we shall instead resolve to a simpler solution based on graph searches. Roughly speaking, we start from the goal conditions to traverse the attack graph backwards by following the directed edges in the reverse direction. During the traversal we make logical inferences. At the end of the graph traversal, a logic proposition of the initial conditions is derived as the necessary and sufficient condition for satisfying the goal. Figure 4.1 shows a procedure *Network_Hardening* that more precisely describes this process.

A line-by-line explanation of procedure *Network_Hardening* shown in Fig. 4.1 is given in the following.

- The first four lines of procedure *Network_Hardening* initialize the result L, a queue Q used for searching the attack graph, and a *predecessor set Pre(x)* for each vertex x (an exploit or a condition) that includes all the vertices reachable from x.
- The procedure then searches the attack graph backwards as follows. For each condition c it leaves (that is, dequeued from Q), it substitutes c in the result L with a logically equivalent proposition, that is, the conjunction of those exploits that imply condition c (line 6 through line 10).
- It expands the search in a breadth-first manner (line 11–12).
- It adds the vertices reachable from the current vertex to the predecessor set of that vertex (line 13).
- The procedure avoids running into cycles by only expanding the search towards those vertices not reachable from the current vertex (line 11), and it also avoids introducing unsatisfiable logic loops into the final result (line 9).
- The procedure handles exploits in a similar way (line 14 through line 21).

To illustrate how the procedure *Network_Hardening* works, we revisit the attack graph and goal condition in Fig. 3.1. Because the procedure will only search among the vertices from which the goal condition is reachable, we can safely remove from further consideration the exploit $local\_bof(1)$ and the condition $root(1)$, together with corresponding edges. The condition $user(0)$, which denotes the attacker's privilege on his/her own machine, can also be removed because it is beyond the control of administrators. The simplified version of the attack graph is shown in Fig. 4.2 (recall that exploits appear as rectangles and conditions as ovals; purple ovals represent initial conditions, whereas blue ovals represent intermediate conditions).

Procedure *Network_Hardening*
Input: Attack graph $G(E \cup C, R_r \cup R_i)$, goal conditions $C_g \subseteq C$
Output: A logic propostion satisfying $\bigwedge_{c \in C_g} \neg c$
Method:

    1. **Let** $L = \bigwedge_{c \in C_g} \neg c$
        //The initial goal
    2. **Let** Q be a queue with the conditions in C_g enqueued
        A queue used for searching in the graph
    3. **For** each $e \in E$ and $c \in C$
    4.   **Let** $Pre(e) = \{e\}$ and $Pre(c) = \{c\}$
        //The predecessor list
    5. **While** Q is not empty, do
    6.   **For** each condition c dequeued from Q, let $S_e = \{e_1, e_2, \ldots, e_n\}$ be the exploits pointing to c in G
    7.   **Let** $T = (e_1 \vee e_2 \vee \ldots e_n)$
        //Temporary variable
    8.   **For** each $e_i \in S_e \cap Pre(c)$
    9.   **Replace** e_i with *FALSE* in T
    10.   **Replace** c with T in L
    11.   **For** each $e_i \in S_e - Pre(c)$
    12.   **Enqueue** e_i in Q
    13.   **Let** $Pre(e_i) = Pre(e_i) \cup Pre(c)$
    14.   **For** each exploit e dequeued from Q, let $S_c = \{c_1, c_2, \ldots, c_m\}$ be the conditions pointing to e in G
    15.   **Let** $T = (c_1 \wedge c_2 \wedge \ldots c_n)$
    16.   **For** each $c_i \in S_c \cap Pre(e)$
    17.   **Replace** c_i with *FALSE* in T
    18.   **Replace** e with T in L
    19.   **For** each $c_i \in S_c - Pre(e)$
    20.   **Enqueue** c_i in Q
    21.   **Let** $Pre(c_i) = Pre(c_i) \cup Pre(e)$
    21. **Return** L

Fig. 4.1 A procedure for Network Hardening

We first consider how the search in the Procedure *Network_Hardening* traverses this attack graph, and we shall show how the result L is updated shortly. Although the search will actually advance breadth-first, we shall describe it in a depth-first manner for clarity. The dotted lines in Fig. 4.2 illustrate how the procedure searches the attack graph. For clarity, we have also divided the search into following steps, which correspond to the labels of the dotted lines in Fig. 4.2.

A: The search starts from the goal condition $root(2)$ and advances to $user(2)$.
B: It branches there and the first branch stops at $ftp(0, 2)$.
C: The other further branches at $ftp\_rhosts(1, 2)$ and the first branch reaches $ftp(1, 2)$.
D: The second branch goes to $user(1)$.
E: Further branches at $user(1)$, and the first upward branch stops at $ftp(0, 1)$.
F: The second upward branch stops at $sshd(0, 1)$.
G: One downward branch goes to $sshd\_bof(2, 1)$ and then stops at $user(2)$, because $user(2)$ is in the predecessor set of $sshd\_bof(2, 1)$.
H: The other downward branch goes to $rsh(2, 1)$ and further branches there.
 I: The first branch stops at $user(2)$, because $user(2)$ is in the predecessor set of $rsh(2, 1)$.
 J: Similarly, the second branch also stops at $user(2)$.

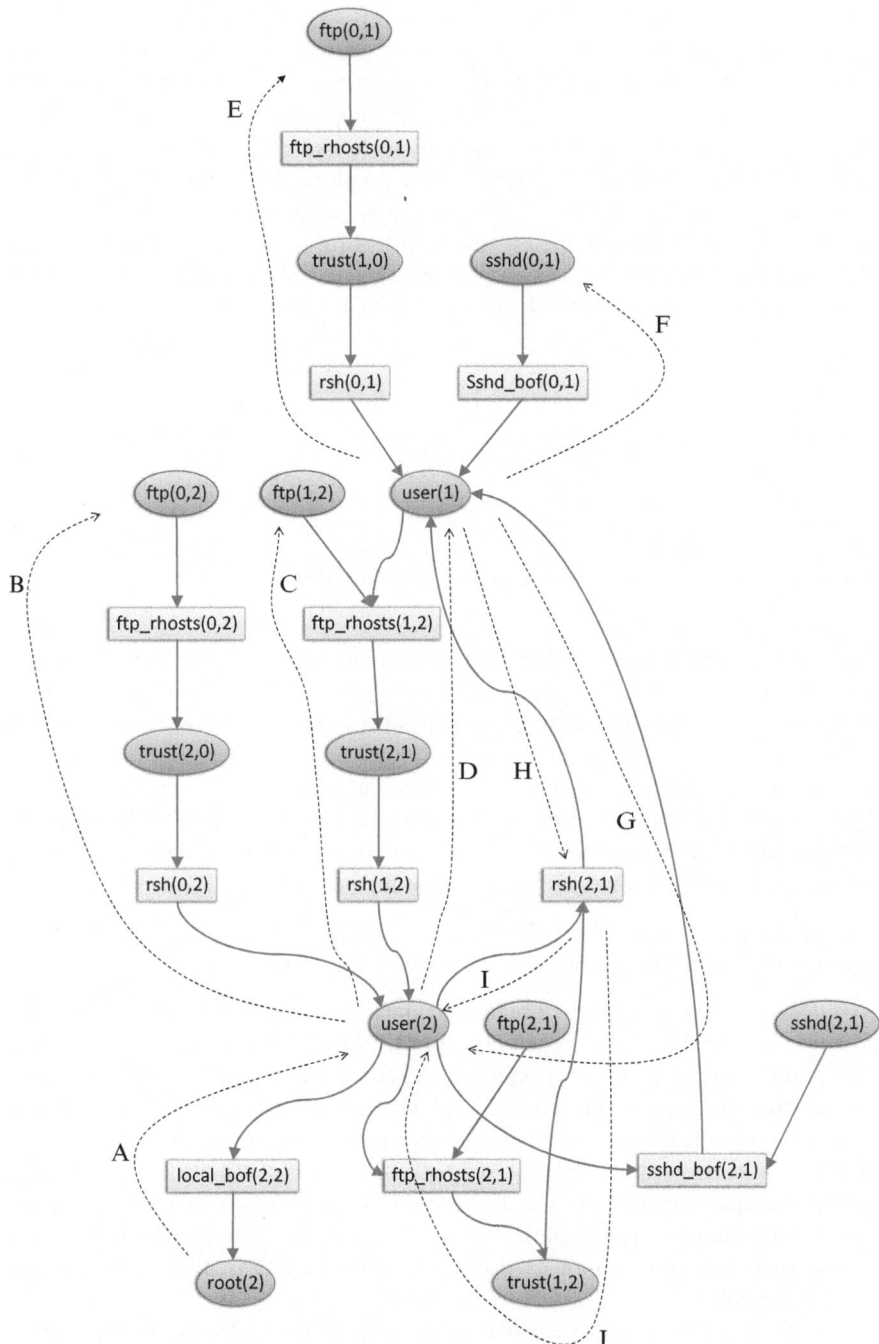

Fig. 4.2 An example of applying procedure *Network_Hardening*

The result L is initially $\neg root(2)$ and is subsequently updated as in Fig. 4.3 (some straightforward steps and parentheses are omitted for simplicity). The condition $user(1)$ actually appears twice in the proposition, required by $rsh(1, 2)$ in line 3 and by $ftp\_rhosts(1, 2)$. The second appearance should be included in line 4 but we have omitted it for simplicity since $user(1) \wedge user(1)$ is logically equivalent to $user(1)$. Notice, however, such simplification is not always possible (for example, in the case of $x \wedge y \vee x \wedge z$, both copies of x must be kept), and it is not part of the procedure. Indeed, the procedure differs from normal breadth-first search (BFS) because it may need to search through a vertex multiple times (for example, x in the case of $x \wedge y \vee x \wedge z$) whereas a BFS visits each vertex exactly once.

1. $L = \neg root(2)$
2. $= \neg(rsh(0, 2) \vee rsh(1, 2))$
3. $= \neg(ftp\_rhosts(0, 2) \vee trust(2, 1) \wedge user(1))$
4. $= \neg(ftp(0, 2) \vee ftp(1, 2) \wedge (rsh(0, 1) \vee sshd\_bof(0, 1) \vee rsh(2, 1) \vee sshd\_bof(2, 1)))$
5. $= \neg(ftp(0, 2) \vee ftp(1, 2) \wedge (ftp(0, 1) \vee sshd(0, 1) \vee trust(1, 2) \wedge FALSE \vee sshd(2, 1) \wedge FALSE))$
6. $= \neg(ftp(0, 2) \vee ftp(1, 2) \wedge (ftp(0, 1) \vee sshd(0, 1) \vee ftp(2, 1) \wedge FALSE \wedge FALSE \vee sshd(2, 1) \wedge FALSE))$
7. $= \neg(ftp(0, 2) \vee ftp(1, 2) \wedge (ftp(0, 1) \vee sshd(0, 1)))$

Fig. 4.3 An example of applying procedure *Network_Hardening*

In Fig. 4.3, the *FALSE* values are results of the two cycles in the attack graph (from $user(1)$ to $user(2)$, through $sshd\_bof(2, 1)$ and through $rsh(2, 1)$, respectively). For example, when the search leaves $rsh(2, 1)$ and reaches $user(2)$, it finds that $user(2)$ is in the predecessor set of $rsh(2, 1)$. Hence, instead of replacing $rsh(2, 1)$ with $user(2) \wedge trust(2, 1)$, line 16 and 17 in Fig. 4.1 replace $rsh(2, 1)$ with $trust(1, 2) \wedge FALSE$. Similar argument explains the other FALSE values in line 5 and line 6. Although we remove the effect of those *FALSE* values in line 7 to simplify the result, note that this is not part of the procedure.

Proposition 4.1. *The procedure* Network_Hardening *shown in Fig. 4.3 returns the necessary and sufficient condition of the given goal condition.*

Proof (Sketch). The correctness of the procedure can be proved by induction on the number of involved exploits. When no exploit is involved, the goal condition must be an initial condition itself, for which the result trivially holds. For the inductive case, suppose the result holds when n exploits are involved. For the case of $n + 1$, considering that the procedure advances in a breadth-first manner, the partial result must hold after n exploits have been processed and the conditions they require have been enqueued (line 14–21). There must be at least one such condition that is implied by the $(n + 1)^{th}$ exploit. We only need to show the procedure correctly expands such a condition into its necessary and sufficient condition through the $(n + 1)^{th}$ exploit.

After the condition is dequeued (line 6), it is replaced by the disjunction of all the exploits that may imply it (including the $(n + 1)^{th}$ exploit), which is the necessary and sufficient condition for the condition to be satisfied (line 7 and 10). However, if an exploit is in the predecessor list of the condition, then realizing the exploit requires the condition to be satisfied in the first place, and hence the exploit should be regarded as unrealizable (an exploit is unrealizable if any of its required conditions is so) and be replaced by *FALSE* (line 9). Next, each of the exploits not in the predecessor list of the condition is enqueued (line 12) and dequeued (line 14) for processing.

Each dequeued exploit is then replaced by its necessary and sufficient condition, that is the conjunction of all the conditions they require (line 15 and 18). However, if a condition is in the predecessor list of the exploit, then the exploit can imply the condition only if the condition is satisfied in the first place. This logic loop implies that this occurrence of the condition in the result should be replaced by *FALSE*. Notice that only this specific occurrence of the condition is set as *FALSE*, but other occurrences of the same condition in the result are not affected. This is because the condition may still be implied by other exploits and hence may still be satisfiable. From the above discussion, the procedure never runs into a loop, and it always terminates with the correct result.   □

4.2.1 Handling Cycles in Attack Graphs

The way we handle cycles in attack graphs is different from that in previous work where cycles are removed through an extra forward search [5]. We do not require such an extra step but avoid cycles in the backward search itself. This simplifies the overall process and helps to avoid complicated situations for handling cycles in an attack graph, as illustrated in the following.

In traversing the attack graph with a forward search [5], we would need to keep track of nodes that are explored (initially no node is explored) such that we would not explore an already explored node when there is a cycle. In addition, we need to keep track of the disabled nodes such that we know when to disable an exploit (when at least one of the required conditions are disabled) or condition (when all of the exploits implying it are disabled). More specifically, a condition should be marked as disabled only if all of the exploits implying it are explored and disabled; it should be marked explored (but not disabled) if all of the exploits implying it are explored but at least one of them is not disabled. Otherwise, we cannot make any decision since the unexplored exploit may or may not be disabled in the future when we explore it. For an exploit, it should be marked as disabled if at least one of the required conditions is disabled; it should be marked explored (but not disabled) if all of the required conditions are explored but not disabled. We cannot make any decision if none of the required conditions is explored.

However, cycles in attack graphs may bring additional difficulties to a forward search. For example, consider the attack graph shown in Fig. 4.4, which includes a cycle $c_5 \rightarrow e_3 \rightarrow c_6 \rightarrow e_4 \rightarrow c_5$. In traversing the graph, after we disable $e1$ and reach c_5, we need to make the decision whether c_5 should be marked as disabled and explored. As aforementioned, we cannot make any decision here since the unexplored exploit e_4 implies c_5 and e_4 may or may not be disabled in the

Fig. 4.4 An example of
cycle in attack graph

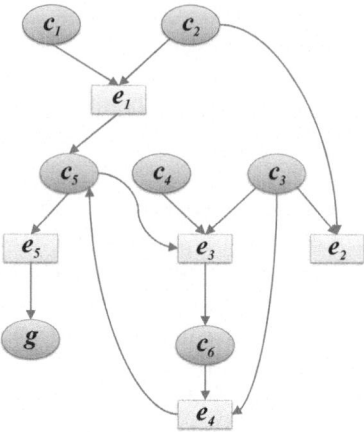

future when we explore it. Similarly, when we proceed from c_3 and c_4 to e_3, since e_3 depends on c_5 that is still not explored, we cannot make any decision. Such an inter-dependency between c_5 and e_4 thus will cause the algorithm to stop. However, we can easily see that in this particular case, e_3 and e_4 can never be exploited if e_1 is disabled. Therefore, we should simply regard all nodes inside the cycle as disabled.

More generally, the following enumerates the different cases we would have to consider in handling cycles during a forward search.

– As illustrated in the upper left-hand side of Fig. 4.5 (0 indicates disabled and 1 not disabled), if we reach a cycle through a condition and if all the exploits required by this condition are not disabled, and if no other exploit from outside the cycle can satisfy the required conditions inside the cycle, then all the nodes will be considered disabled.
– As illustrated in the upper right-hand side of Fig. 4.5, if we reach a cycle through a condition and if all the exploits required by this condition are not disabled, and if any other exploit from outside the cycle can satisfy the required condition inside the cycle, then all the nodes will be considered not disabled.
– As illustrated in the lower left-hand side of Fig. 4.5, if we reach a cycle through an exploit and if all the conditions required by this exploit are not disabled, and if no other exploit from outside the cycle can satisfy the required condition inside the cycle, then all the nodes will be considered disabled.
– As illustrated in the lower right-hand side of Fig. 4.5, if we reach a cycle through an exploit and if all the conditions which required by this exploit are not explored, and if any other exploit from outside the cycle can satisfy the required condition inside the cycle, then all the nodes will be considered not disabled.

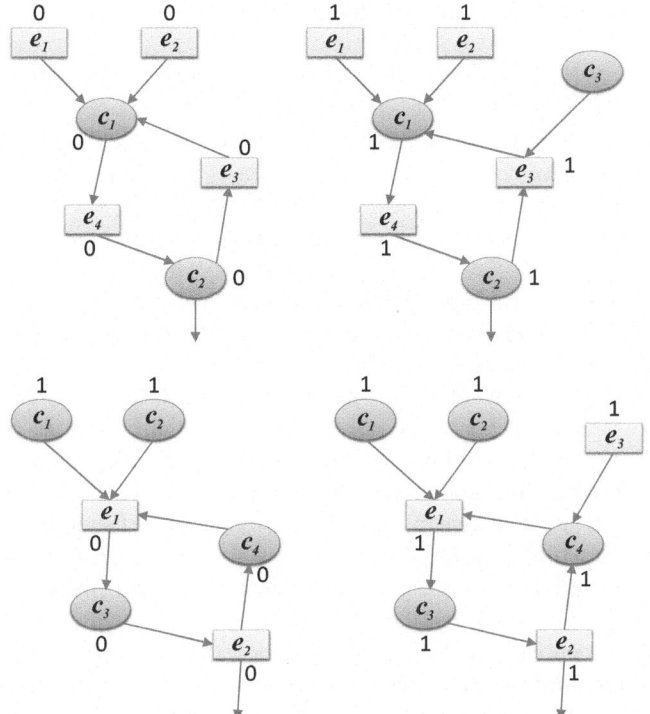

Fig. 4.5 Different cases of cycles

4.3   Choosing Minimum-Cost Solutions

By Definition 3.3, a logic proposition L returned by the procedure *Network_Hardening* is the necessary and sufficient condition for hardening the network such that none of the goal conditions can be satisfied. However, such a proposition usually implies multiple non-comparable options. Moreover, such options are not always so apparent from the proposition itself. Therefore, we go even further to simplify the proposition and choose optimal solutions with respect to given cost metrics.

We first convert the proposition L returned by the Procedure *Network_Hardening* to its disjunctive normal form (DNF). Each disjunction in the DNF thus represents a particular sufficient option in hardening the network. Because each disjunction in the DNS is the conjunction of negated initial conditions, those initial conditions must be disabled. This is enforceable, because all the initial conditions are independent of others and can be readily disabled. For example, from the last line in Fig. 4.3 we have the following.

$$L = \neg(ftp(0, 2) \vee ftp(1, 2) \wedge (ftp(0, 1) \vee sshd(0, 1)))$$

We can convert L to its DNF as follows. First,

$$L \equiv \neg((ftp(0,2) \vee ftp(1,2)) \wedge (ftp(0,2) \vee ftp(0,1) \vee sshd(0,1)))$$

holds by the tautology $A \vee B \wedge C \leftrightarrow (A \vee B) \wedge (A \vee C)$ [4]. Then by applying De Morgan's law, we have

$$L \equiv \neg ftp(0,2) \wedge \neg ftp(1,2) \vee \neg ftp(0,2) \wedge \neg ftp(0,1) \wedge \neg sshd(0,1)$$

From this DNF, we clearly know the two options in hardening the network: one is to disable both $ftp(0,2)$ and $ftp(1,2)$, the other is to disable the three conditions $ftp(0,2)$, $ftp(0,1)$, and $sshd(0,1)$.

However, although any of the disjunctions in the DNF of L is a sufficient option for hardening the network, the cost of those options may be different. First, the set of initial conditions involved in one option may be a proper super set of those involved in another option. The cost incurred by the latter option is clearly no greater than that by the former, and hence the former option can be removed from further consideration. Figure 4.6 shows an example of attack graph with two initial conditions. The Procedure *Network_Hardening* will return $L = \neg((c_1 \vee c_2) \wedge c_1 \wedge c_2)$, and the DNF is $L \equiv \neg c_1 \wedge \neg c_2 \vee \neg c_1 \vee \neg c_2$. Clearly, among the three options $\neg c_1 \wedge \neg c_2$, $\neg c_1$, and $\neg c_2$, the first incurs no less cost than the second or the third and hence should be removed from consideration.

The above example also shows that theoretically the DNF of L may have an exponential size in the number of initial conditions (after the above reduction, this number of options will be bound by the number of incomparable subsets of n initial conditions, which is known as the binomial coefficient $\binom{n}{\lfloor n/2 \rfloor}$ by Sperner's Theorem). This implies that the Procedure *Network_Hardening* has an unavoidable exponential worst-case complexity, because its result is exponential. Indeed, the procedure may visit a vertex many times (bound by the in-degree of the vertex). However, based on our experiences we believe in practice the running time is

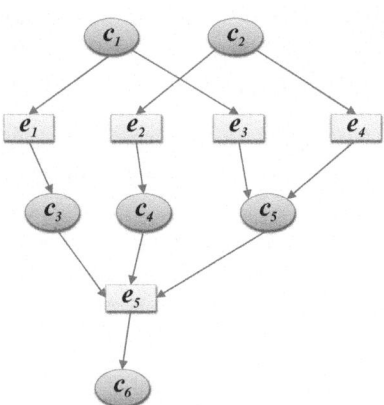

Fig. 4.6 An example of attack graph with exponential number of hardening options

usually acceptable. This is because the attack graph of a well-protected network is usually small and sparse (the in-degree of each vertex is small) since most easy-to-remove vulnerabilities have already been disabled through existing security measures such as firewalls. Attack graph analysis is less useful for unsecured networks, in which the analysis conclusion is simply "harden everything." It is more useful in situations where some basic network hardening has already been done, and careful analysis is needed for evaluating risk versus hardening cost in the context of multi-step attacks. Nonetheless, we will present heuristic methods in next chapter to tackle this scalability issue.

After the above reduction, the options left will only involve pairwise incomparable subsets of initial conditions. The options that incur the minimum cost can be easily chosen, if the cost of disabling each initial condition has been assigned by administrators. In such a case, the cost of an option is simply equal to the summation of the cost of all the initial conditions involved by the option. Although it is usually difficult to assign precise cost to each condition, the conditions can always be partially ordered based on their costs. Consequently, the options can also be partially ordered based on the cost of conditions. An option with a cost no greater than any other options can thus be chosen based on the partial order.

For example, consider the two options we have derived, that is either to disable both $ftp(0, 2)$ and $ftp(1, 2)$, or to disable the three conditions $ftp(0, 2)$, $ftp(0, 1)$, and $sshd(0, 1)$. The condition $ftp(0, 2)$ must be disabled in either case, and hence it can be ignored in considering relative costs. Since the condition $sshd(0, 1)$ can be disabled by patching the buffer overflow vulnerability in the sshd service, the cost may be relatively low. On the other hand, the conditions involving the ftp service incurs more costs, because the ftp service is properly functioning, and is simply used by the attacker in a clever way. Moreover, disabling $ftp(0, 2)$ may mean stopping the ftp service on host 2 to all external hosts, which may incur a higher cost than stopping the ftp service between two internal hosts 1 and 2 (they may still communicate files via other services). Based on those assumptions, the first option has a lower cost than that of the second and thus should be chosen as the solution.

4.4 Case Study

In this section we study a relatively more realistic example with enhanced security measures as well as attacks at multiple network layers (similar to the example in [5]). The example discussed in previous sections has focused on the Procedure *Network_Hardening*, whereas this second example will better justify our techniques in choosing the minimum-cost network hardening option as discussed in the previous section. Moreover, this example more clearly reveals the limitations of existing approaches, such as the minimum critical set approach [3, 6] and the set of all reachable exploits [1].

Figure 4.7 shows the network configuration for our second example. The link-layer connectivity between the three hosts is provided by an Ethernet switch. At the transport layer, security has been enhanced by removing unused services, replacing FTP and telnet with secure shell, and adding tcpwrapper protection on RPC services. Application-layer trust relationships further restrict NFS and NIS domain access. In spite of those security measures, exploits still exist and are listed in Table 4.1, whereas security conditions are listed in Table 4.2. Figure 4.8 then shows the attack graph for this example. The lowercase Greek letters are used as short names for the corresponding initial conditions. Notice that we allow some of the conditions to have multiple copies to keep the attack graph legible. Also, the conditions are used as labels of edges between exploits for simplicity.

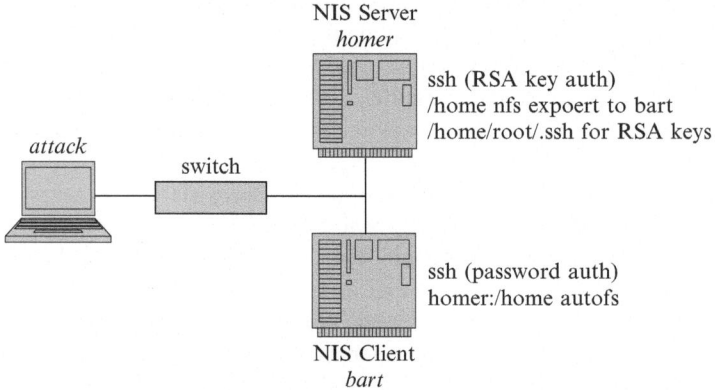

Fig. 4.7 Network configuration for second example

Table 4.1 Exploits for the second example

Exploit	Description
arp_spoof	Spoof (impersonate) machine identity via ARP poison attack
ypcat_passwd	Dump encrypted NIS password file
crack_yp_passwd	Crack encrypted user password(s)
scp_upload_pw	Secure shell copy, upload direction, using password authentication
scp_download_pw	Secure shell copy, download direction, using password authentication
ssh_login_pw	Secure shell login using password authentication
rh62_glibc_bof	Red Hat 6.2 buffer overflow in glibc library
create_nfs_home_ssh_pk_su	Exploit NFS home share to create secure shell key pair used for superuser authentication
ssh_login_pk_su	Secure shell login using public key authentication

Table 4.2 Security conditions for the second example

Condition	Description
link_arp	Attacker shares link-level connectivity with victim (both on same LAN)
trans_yp	Transport layer connectivity to NIS server
trans_ssh_pw	Transport layer connectivity to secure shell server that supports password authentication
trans_ssh_pk	Transport layer connectivity to secure shell server that supports public key authentication
trans_nfs	Transport layer connectivity to NFS server
app_nfs_home_su	Application "connection" representing sharing superuser's home directory
app_yp_domain	Application "connection" representing NIS domain membership
app_yp_passwd	Application "connection" representing acquisition of encrypted NIS password database
app_pwauth	Application "connection" representing acquisition of unencrypted user password
app_ssh_pk_su	Application "connection" representing acquisition/creation of key pair for superuser authentication
pgm_glibc_bof	Program used to exploit glibc library buffer overflow vulnerability
execute	Execute access obtained
superuser	Superuser privilege obtained

The Procedure *Network_Hardening* searches the attack graph in a way similar to the previous example. The search starts from the goal conditions and branches at the exploit $ssh\_login\_pk\_su(bart, homer)$. The right branch ends at the condition η. The middle branch reaches the exploit $ssh\_login\_pw(attack, bart)$ and consequently ends at the conditions α, β, χ. The left branch further branches at the exploit $create\_nfs\_home\_ssh\_pk\_su(bart, homer)$. The middle two branches reach the conditions ϕ and γ. The right branch reaches $ssh\_login\_pw(attack, bart)$ for the second time and advances as usual. The left branch reaches the condition $pgm\_glibc\_bof(bart)$ and further branches there. The right branch reaches conditions δ and ε, and also the exploit $ssh\_login\_pw(attack, bart)$ for the third time. The left branch reaches α, β, and χ via the exploit $scp\_upload\_pw(attack, bart)$.

The result returned by the procedure is thus

$$T = \neg(\eta \wedge (\phi \wedge \gamma) \wedge (\alpha \wedge \beta \wedge \chi) \wedge ((\alpha \wedge \beta \wedge \chi) \vee (\alpha \wedge \beta \wedge \chi \wedge \delta \wedge \varepsilon)))$$

(some parentheses are omitted for simplicity). This seemingly complex result, however, has a simple DNF

$$\neg\alpha \vee \neg\beta \vee \neg\chi \vee \neg\phi \vee \neg\gamma \vee \neg\eta$$

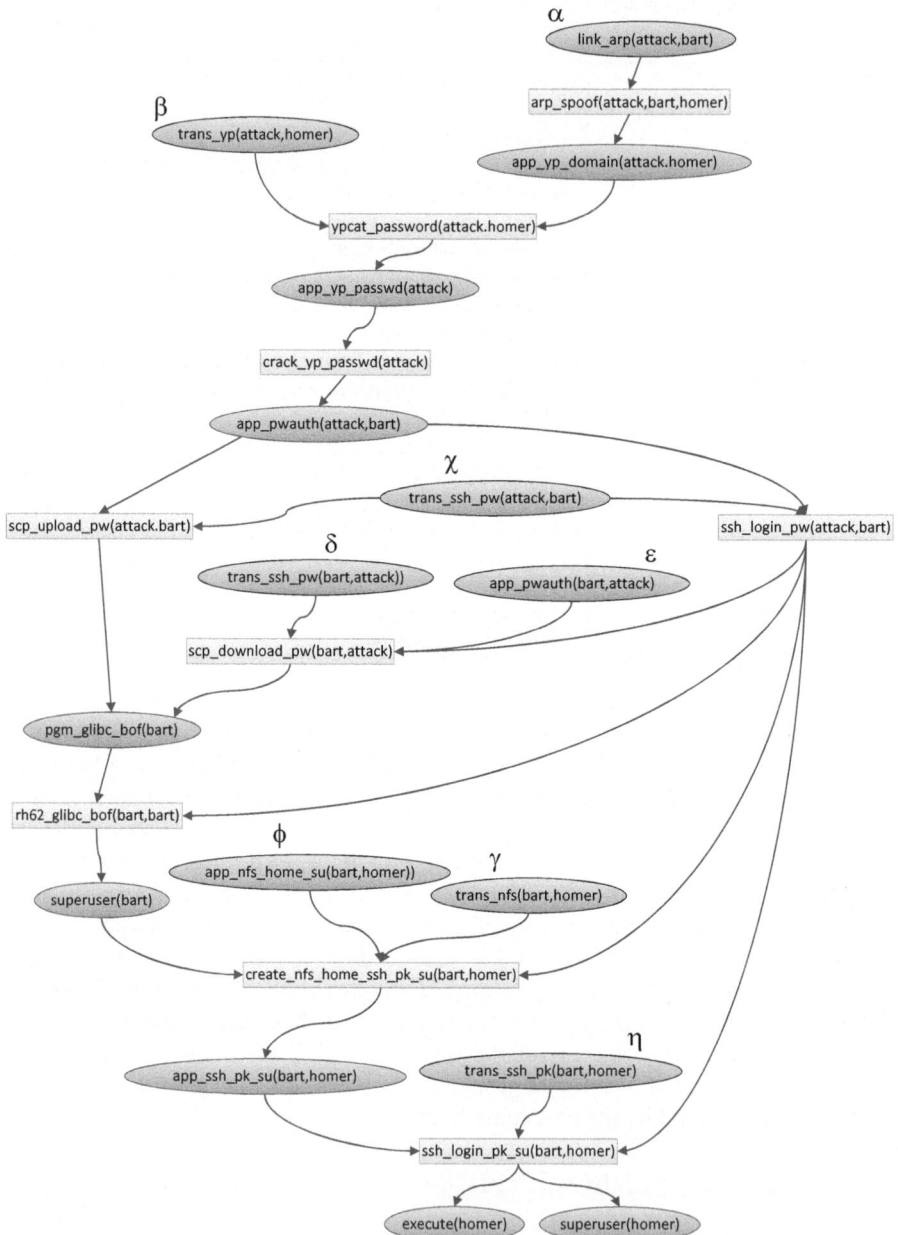

Fig. 4.8 Attack graph for the second example

The two initial conditions δ and ε do not appear in the DNF. They have dropped out in this fashion:

$$(\alpha \wedge \beta \wedge \chi) \vee (\alpha \wedge \beta \wedge \chi \wedge \delta \wedge \varepsilon) \equiv \alpha \wedge \beta \wedge \chi$$

due to tautology $A \vee (A \wedge B) \leftrightarrow A$. Intuitively, the condition $pgm\_glibc\_bof(bart)$ is implied by either $scp\_upload\_pw(attack, bart)$ or $scp\_download\_pw$ $(bart, attack)$. The latter requires two more conditions, δ and ε, than the former does. Therefore, disabling δ and ε does not help at all.

It is worth noting that the above important observation would be difficult if at all possible with the exploit-based approaches [1, 3, 6]. First, the goal conditions are reachable from both δ and ε, and hence a reachability-based algorithm will not detect their irrelevancy to network hardening. If such conditions are not initial conditions but the ends of another chain of exploits, then whatever initial conditions the chain lead to will be erroneously disabled, causing unnecessary loss of availability. Second, any singleton set of exploits except $scp\_upload\_pw(attack, bart)$ and $scp\_download\_pw(bart, attack)$ comprises a minimum critical set in this case, and the set $\{scp\_upload\_pw(attack, bart), scp\_download\_pw(bart, attack)\}$ is a minimal critical set. However, such a result is not as clear as our result, considering the fact that some of the exploits cannot be directly removed, such as $crack\_yp\_passwd(attack)$ and $rh62\_glibc\_bof(bart, bart)$.

The six network hardening options we now have are:

1. $\neg link\_arp(attack, bart)$, or
2. $\neg trans\_yp(attack, homer)$, or
3. $\neg trans\_ssh\_pw(attack, bart)$, or
4. $\neg app\_nfs\_home\_su(bart, homer)$, or
5. $\neg trans\_nfs(bart, homer)$, or
6. $\neg trans\_ssh\_pk(bart, homer)$

Those options can be partially ordered with the following assumptions about the cost of each initial condition.

– For the first option, $link\_arp$ refers to mapping IP addresses to MAC addresses through ARP (address resolution protocol). Therefore, the first option can be enforced by hard-coding IP/MAC address and switching port relationships throughout the network, which clearly incurs management overhead costs.
– For the third option, the condition $trans\_ssh\_pw(attack, bart)$ can be disabled by modifying the sshd configuration of the host $bart$ to use public-key authentication only (disabling password authentication). This enhances security and is thus a low-cost option (which is actually already in place for the host $homer$).
– For the fourth option, $app\_nfs\_home\_su(bart, homer)$ is an application-layer association that represents the sharing of the superuser home directory. Although such configuration may ease administration, it is indeed a poor practice from a security viewpoint (it allows the overwriting of a secure shell authentication key pair in this particular case). Therefore, the fourth option incurs some administration cost and can be enforced by removing the directory share.

– On the other hand, the remaining three options (the second, fifth, and sixth option) would make critical network services unavailable and thus incur high costs in terms of availability.

From the above discussion, we conclude with a partial order of the six options based on their relative costs: $3 < 1, 4 < 2, 5, 6$. That is, the third option is the minimum-cost solution to network hardening.

4.5   Summary

In this chapter, we have proposed methods to compute network hardening options for protecting given critical resources. We have also discussed how to choose hardening options with the minimum cost. Unlike previous approaches, the network hardening solutions we provided were in terms of adjustable network configuration elements rather than exploits. Such solutions took into account the often complex relationships among exploits and configuration elements. In this way, our solution was readily enforceable, and it kept the cost of network hardening minimal by leaving out those seemingly irrelevant exploits whose removal actually had no effect on protecting critical resources. Unlike the previous work, the algorithm we proposed could derive solutions with one-pass of search in the attack graph while avoiding logic loops. This not only saved an unnecessary preprocessing step, but also addressed the difficulty in handling different types of cycles. The current algorithm builds the logic proposition then simplifies it. One further improvement would be to pursue a solution that integrates the two steps into one single algorithm such that redundant clauses in the proposition can be avoided.

References

1. P. Ammann, D. Wijesekera, and S. Kaushik.   Scalable, graph-based network vulnerability analysis. In *Proceedings of ACM CCS'02*, 2002.
2. R. Deraison. Nessus scanner, 1999. Available at http://www.nessus.org.
3. S. Jha, O. Sheyner, and J.M. Wing. Two formal analysis of attack graph. In *Proceedings of the 15th Computer Security Foundation Workshop (CSFW'02)*, 2002.
4. E. Mendelson. *Introduction to Mathematical Logic, 4th ed.* Chapman & Hall, 1997.
5. S. Noel, S. Jajodia, B. O'Berry, and M. Jacobs. Efficient minimum-cost network hardening via exploit dependency grpahs. In *Proceedings of the 19th Annual Computer Security Applications Conference (ACSAC'03)*, 2003.
6. O. Sheyner, J. Haines, S. Jha, R. Lippmann, and J.M. Wing. Automated generation and analysis of attack graphs. In *Proceedings of the IEEE S&P'02*, 2002.

Chapter 5
Linear-Time Network Hardening

Abstract Attack graph analysis has been established as a powerful tool for analyzing network vulnerability. However, previous approaches to network hardening look for exact solutions and thus do not scale. Further, hardening elements have been treated independently, which is inappropriate for real environments. For example, the cost for patching many systems may be nearly the same as for patching a single one. Or patching a vulnerability may have the same effect as blocking traffic with a firewall, while blocking a port may deny legitimate service. By failing to account for such hardening interdependencies, the resulting recommendations can be unrealistic and far from optimal. Instead, we formalize the notion of hardening strategy in terms of allowable actions, and define a cost model that takes into account the impact of interdependent hardening actions. We also introduce a near-optimal approximation algorithm that scales linearly with the size of the graphs, which we validate experimentally.

5.1 Overview

As the previous chapter has shown, attack graph analysis can be extended to automatically generate recommendations for hardening networks. One must consider combinations of network conditions to harden, which has corresponding impact on removing paths in the attack graph. Further, one can generate hardening solutions that are optimal with respect to some notion of cost. Such hardening solutions prevent the attack from succeeding, while minimizing the associated costs.

However, as it has been shown, the general solution to optimal network hardening scales exponentially as the number of hardening options itself scales exponentially with the size of the attack graph. In applying network hardening to realistic network environments, it is crucial that the algorithms are able to scale. Progress has been made in reducing the complexity of attack graph manipulation so that it scales

L. Wang et al., *Network Hardening: An Automated Approach to Improving Network Security*, SpringerBriefs in Computer Science, DOI 10.1007/978-3-319-04612-9__5,

quadratically (linearly within defined security zones) [1]. However, the previous approach to generating hardening recommendations searches for exact solutions, which is inherently an intractable problem.

Another limitation of the previous technique is the assumption that network conditions are hardened independently. This assumption does not hold true in real network environments. Realistically, network administrators can take actions that affect vulnerabilities across the network, such as pushing patches out to many systems at once. Further, the same hardening result may be obtained through more than one action. Overall, to provide realistic recommendations, our hardening strategy must take such factors into account.

In this chapter, we remove the assumption of independent hardening actions. Instead, we define a network hardening strategy as a set of allowable atomic actions that involve hardening multiple network conditions. We introduce a formal cost model that accounts for the impact of these hardening actions. This allows the definition of hardening costs that accurately reflect realistic network environments. Because computing the minimum-cost hardening solution is intractable, we introduce an approximation algorithm for optimal hardening. This algorithm finds near-optimal solutions while scaling almost linearly—for certain values of the parameters—with the size of the attack graph, which we validate experimentally. Finally, we determine the theoretical upper bound for the worst-case approximation ratio, and show that, in practice, the approximation ratio is much lower than such bound.

The chapter is organized as follows. Section 5.2 provides a motivating example. Then Sect. 5.3 introduces the proposed cost model, and Sect. 5.4 describes our approach to time-efficient and cost-effective network hardening. Finally, Sect. 5.5 reports experimental results, and Sect. 5.6 gives some concluding remarks and indicates further research directions.

5.2 Motivating Example

Figure 5.1 repeats our running example of attack graph (recall that exploits appear as rectangles and conditions as ovals; purple ovals represent initial conditions, whereas blue ovals represent intermediate conditions). Recall that some modeling simplifications have been made, such as combining transport-layer ftp connectivity between two hosts h_s and h_d, physical-layer connectivity, and the existence of the ftp daemon on host h_d into a single condition $ftp(h_s, h_d)$. In this example, we assume that our objective is to harden the network with respect to target condition $root(2)$, i.e., we want to prevent the attacker from gaining root privileges on host 2.

Again, although the scenario depicted in Fig. 5.1 is relatively simple (with three hosts—denoted host 0, 1, and 2 respectively—and four types of vulnerabilities—$ftp\_rhosts, rsh, sshd\_bof$, and $local\_bof$), because multiple interleaved attack paths can lead to the goal condition, an optimal solution to harden the network is still not apparent from the attack graph itself, and finding such a solution by hand may not be trivial. Recall that, the following are some of the valid attack paths.

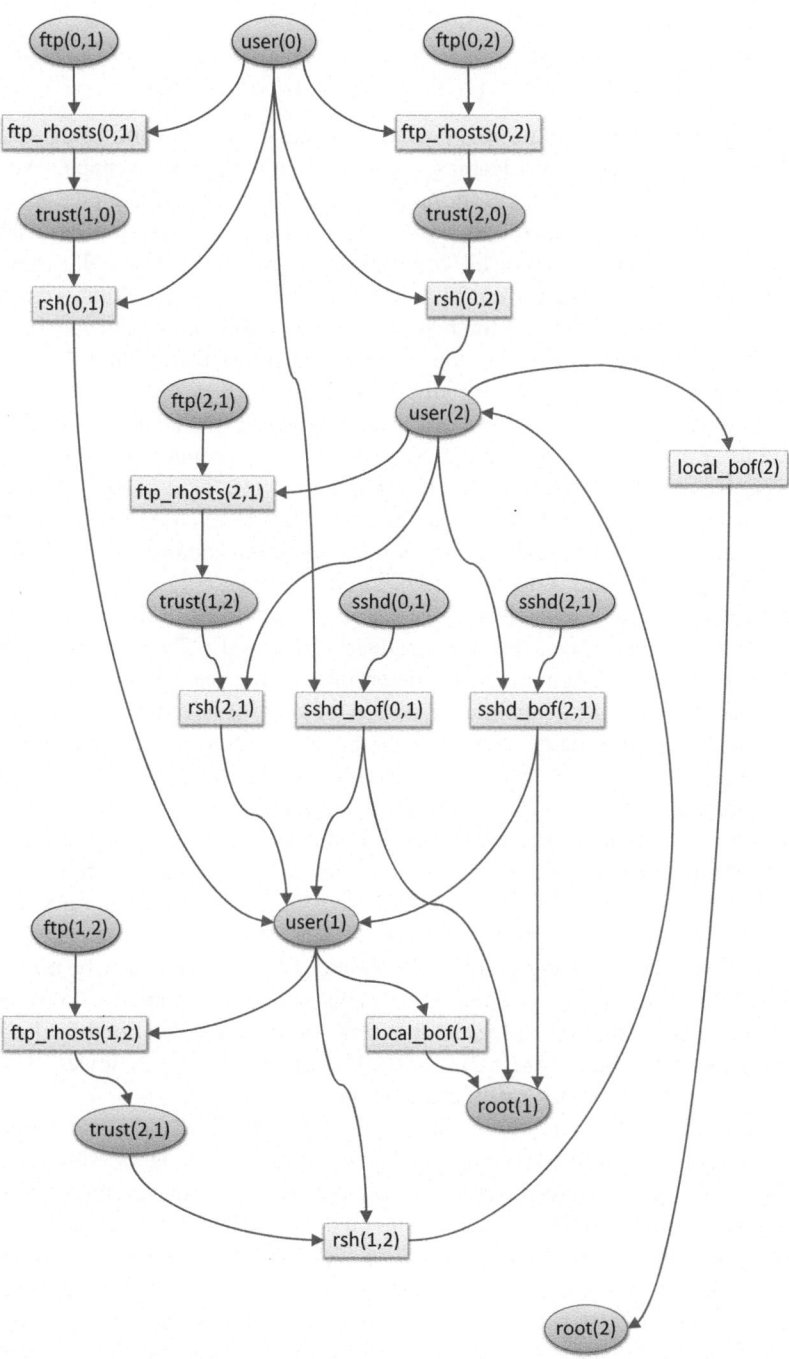

Fig. 5.1 The running example of attack graph

- $ftp\_rhosts(0, 2), rsh(0, 2), local\_bof(2)$
- $ftp\_rhosts(0, 1), rsh(0, 1), ftp\_rhosts(1, 2), rsh(1, 2), local\_bof(2)$
- $sshd\_bof(0, 2), ftp\_rhosts(1, 2), rsh(1, 2), local\_bof(2)$

Although an intuitive solution to prevent the goal condition from being satisfied is to break all the attack paths leading to the goal, in the previous chapter we have seen that such a solution ignores the important fact that not all exploits are under the direct control of administrators. An exploit can only be removed by disabling its required conditions, but not all conditions can be disabled at will. That is, a consequence cannot be removed without removing its causes. Some conditions are implied by other exploits. Such intermediate conditions cannot be independently disabled without removing the exploits that imply them. Only those initial conditions that are not implied by any exploit can be disabled independently of other exploits. Hence, it is important to distinguish between these two kinds of conditions. For instance, in Fig. 5.1, exploit $rsh(1, 2)$ cannot be independently removed, because the two conditions it requires, $trust(2, 1)$ and $user(1)$, are both intermediate conditions and cannot be independently disabled. For this reason, the approach proposed in the previous chapter relies on initial conditions only. However, it also has some limitations that we address in this chapter.

First of all, this approach has no explicit cost model and assumes that each initial condition can be independently disabled. Thus, even when all possible solutions are enumerated, determining the one with the minimum cost is based either on a qualitative notion of cost or on simply counting the conditions that need to be disabled. For the attack graph of Fig. 5.1, the algorithm introduced in the previous chapter returns two solutions, $\{ftp(0, 2), ftp(1, 2)\}$ and $\{ftp(0, 2), ftp(0, 1), sshd(0, 1)\}$. At this point, there is no clear procedure to decide which solution has the minimum cost, unless we make the assumption that the cost of removing each individual condition is assigned by administrators.

Intuitively, one may expect the solution $\{ftp(0, 2), ftp(1, 2)\}$ to have a lower cost than $\{ftp(0, 2), ftp(0, 1), sshd(0, 1)\}$, as fewer conditions need to be disabled. However, removing both $ftp(0, 2)$ and $ftp(1, 2)$ may only be possible if the ftp service on host 2 is shut down. This action may have a considerable cost in terms of disruption to legitimate users. In this case, the combined cost of removing the conditions $\{ftp(0, 2), ftp(0, 1), sshd(0, 1)\}$ may be lower, as it may be achieved by simply blocking all traffic from host 0.

To conclude, note that the attack graph of Fig. 5.1 has the same hardening solutions as the simplified attack graph of Fig. 5.2. This is possible because the algorithm discussed in the previous chapter traverses the graph from target conditions to initial conditions, and, relying on the monotonicity assumption, breaks all the cycles. Intuitively, from the point of view of a target condition, the attack graph can be seen as a tree rooted at the target condition and having initial conditions as the leaf nodes. In fact, each condition is *implied* by one or more exploits. In turn, each exploit *requires* one or more preconditions to be satisfied. We leverage this observation in our approach to network hardening.

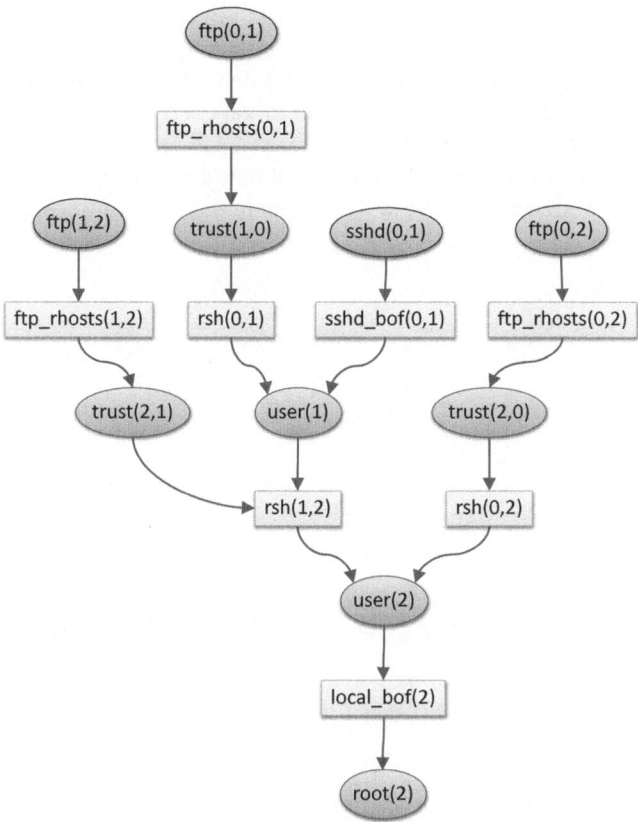

Fig. 5.2 A tree-style attack graph equivalent to the graph of Fig. 5.1 w.r.t. target condition $root(2)$

5.3   Cost Model

Disabling a set of initial conditions in order to prevent attacks on given targets may result in undesired effects, such as denial of service to legitimate users. These effects are greatly amplified when initial conditions cannot be individually disabled, but rather require actions that disable a larger number of conditions. In the following, we define a *network hardening strategy* as a set of atomic actions that can be taken to harden a network.

For instance, an allowable hardening action may consist in stopping ftp service on a given host. Thus, each action may have additional effects besides disabling a desired condition. Such effects must be taken into account when computing minimum-cost solutions. Previous work simply assumes that initial conditions can be individually disabled. We take a more general approach and therefore drop this assumption. For instance, in the attack graph of Fig. 5.1, disabling $ftp(1, 2)$ might not be possible without also disabling $ftp(0, 2)$.

Definition 5.1 (Allowable Hardening Action). Given an attack graph $G = (E \cup C, R_r \cup R_i)$, an *allowable hardening action* (or simply *hardening action*) A is any subset of the set C_i of initial conditions such that all the conditions in A can be jointly disabled in a single step, and no other initial condition $c \in C_i \setminus A$ is disabled when conditions in A are disabled.

A hardening action A is said to be minimal if and only if $\nexists A^* \subset A$ s.t. A^* is an allowable hardening action. We use $\mathscr{A}$ to denote the set of all possible hardening actions.

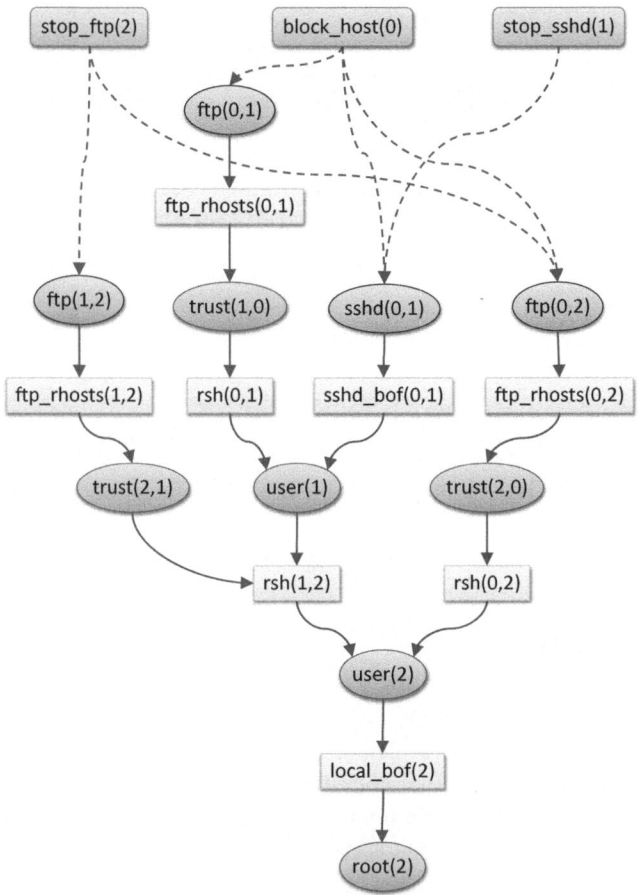

Fig. 5.3 Possible hardening actions (*orange rectangles*) for the attack graph of Fig. 5.2 (Color figure online)

Figure 5.3 depicts the same attack graph of Fig. 5.2, but it explicitly shows the allowable hardening actions, represented as rounded rectangles. Dashed edges indicate which conditions are disabled by each action. Intuitively, a network hardening action is an *atomic* step that network administrators can take to harden the network (e.g., closing an ftp port). When an action A is taken, all and only the conditions in A are removed.[1] In the example of Fig. 5.3, $\mathscr{A} = \{stop\_ftp(2),$ $block\_host(0),$ $stop\_sshd(1)\}$, $stop\_ftp(2)$ $=$ $\{ftp(0, 2),$ $ftp(1, 2)\}$, $block\_host(0)$ $=$ $\{ftp(0, 1),$ $sshd(0, 1),$ $ftp(0, 2)\}$, and $stop\_sshd(1)$ $=$ $\{sshd(0, 1)\}$. In this example, the condition $ftp(1, 2)$ cannot be individually disabled, and can only be disabled by taking action $stop\_ftp(2)$, which also disables $ftp(0, 2)$.[2]

Therefore, when choosing a set of initial conditions to be removed in order to prevent attacks on given targets, we should take into account all the implications of removing those conditions. Removing specific initial conditions may require to take actions that disable additional conditions, including conditions not explicitly modeled in the attack graph, such as conditions that are not part of any attack path. To address this problem, we formalize the notion of hardening strategy in terms of allowable actions, and define a cost model that takes into account the impact of hardening actions. This novel approach improves the state of the art, while preserving the key idea that solutions are truly enforceable only if they operate on initial conditions.

First, we drop the assumption that initial conditions can be individually disabled. In our framework, this simplifying assumption corresponds to the special case where, for each initial condition, there exists an allowable action that disables that condition only, i.e., $(\forall c \in C_i)(\exists A \in \mathscr{A})A = \{c\}$. We then define the notion of *network hardening strategy* in terms of allowable actions.

Definition 5.2 (Network Hardening Strategy). Given an attack graph $G = (E \cup C, R_r \cup R_i)$, a set $\mathscr{A}$ of allowable actions, and a set of target conditions $C_t = \{c_1, \ldots, c_n\}$, a *network hardening strategy* (or simply *hardening strategy*) S is a set of network hardening actions $\{A_1, \ldots, A_m\}$ s.t. conditions $c_1, \ldots, c_n$ cannot be reached after all the actions in S have been taken. We use $\mathscr{S}$ to denote the set of all possible strategies, and $C(S)$ to denote the set of all the conditions disabled under strategy S, i.e., $C(S) = \bigcup_{A \in S} A$.

Intuitively, a hardening strategy is a set of allowable actions breaking all attack paths leading to the target conditions.

We now introduce a cost model, enabling a more accurate analysis of available hardening options.

Definition 5.3 (Hardening Cost Function).

A *hardening cost function* is any function $cost : \mathscr{S} \to \mathbb{R}^+$ that satisfies the following axioms:

---

[1] In practice, an action may also remove conditions not explicitly modeled in the attack graph, and this should be taken into account when assigning a cost to each action.

[2] More precisely, all conditions of the form $ftp(x, 2)$, where x is any host, are disabled by action $stop\_ftp(2)$.

$$cost(\emptyset) = 0 \tag{5.1}$$

$$(\forall S_1, S_2 \in \mathscr{S}) \, (C(S_1) \subseteq C(S_2) \;\Rightarrow\; cost(S_1) \le cost(S_2)) \tag{5.2}$$

$$(\forall S_1, S_2 \in \mathscr{S}) \, (cost(S_1 \cup S_2) \le cost(S_1) + cost(S_2)) \tag{5.3}$$

In other words, the above definition requires that (1) the cost of the empty strategy—the one not removing any condition—is 0; (2) if the set of conditions disabled under S_1 is a subset of the conditions disabled under S_2, then the cost of S_1 is less than or equal to the cost of S_2 (monotonicity); and (3) the cost of the combined strategy $S_1 \cup S_2$ is less than or equal to the sum of the individual costs of S_1 and S_2 (triangular inequality).

Combining the three axioms above, we can conclude that $(\forall S_1, S_2 \in \mathscr{S}) \, (0 \le \max(cost(S_1), cost(S_2)) \le (cost(S_1 \cup S_2) \le cost(S_1) + cost(S_2))$.

A cost function is said to be *additive* if and only if the following additional axiom is satisfied.

$$(\forall S_1, S_2 \in \mathscr{S})(S_1 \cap S_2 = \emptyset \iff cost(S_1) + cost(S_2) = cost(S_1 \cup S_2)) \tag{5.4}$$

Many different cost functions may be defined. The following is a very simple cost function:

$$cost_a(S) = |C(S)| \tag{5.5}$$

The above cost function simply counts the initial conditions that are removed under a network hardening strategy S, and clearly satisfies the three axioms of Definition 5.3. If actions in $\mathscr{A}$ are pairwise disjoint, then $cost_a$ is also additive.

5.4   Network Hardening

In this section, we first examine in more details the limitations of the approach proposed in the previous chapter, and then introduce our approximation algorithm to find reasonably good hardening strategies in a time efficient manner.

5.4.1   Limitations of Previous Approach

The algorithm presented in the previous chapter starts from a set C_t of target conditions and traverses the attack graph backwards, making logical inferences. At the end of the graph traversal, a logic proposition of the initial conditions is derived as the necessary and sufficient condition for hardening the network with respect to C_t. This proposition then needs to be converted to its disjunctive normal form (DNF), with each disjunction in the DNF representing a particular

---

Algorithm 1 $BackwardSearch(G, C_t)$

Input: Attack graph $G = (E \cup C, R_r \cup R_i)$, and set of target conditions C_t.
Output: Optimal hardening strategy.
 1: // Initialize the set of all solutions and iterate until solutions contain initial conditions only
 2: $\mathscr{S} \leftarrow \{C_t\}$
 3: **while** $(\exists S \in \mathscr{S})(S \nsubseteq C_i)$ **do**
 4:     // Replace each non-initial condition with the set of exploits that imply it
 5:     **for all** $S \in \mathscr{S}$ **do**
 6:         **for all** $c \in S$ s.t. $c \notin C_i$ **do**
 7:             $S \leftarrow S \setminus \{c\} \cup \{e \in E \mid (e, c) \in R_i\}$
 8:         **end for**
 9:     **end for**
10:     // Replace exploits with required conditions and generate all possible combinations
11:     **for all** $S = \{e_1, \ldots, e_m\} \in \mathscr{S}$ **do**
12:         $\mathscr{S} \leftarrow \mathscr{S} \setminus \{S\} \cup \{\{c_1, \ldots, c_m\} \mid (\forall i \in [1, m]) \, (c_i, e_i) \in R_r\}$
13:     **end for**
14: **end while**
15: // Replace initial conditions with allowable actions and generate all possible combinations
16: **for all** $S = \{c_1, \ldots, c_n\} \in \mathscr{S}$ **do**
17:     $\mathscr{S} \leftarrow \mathscr{S} \setminus \{S\} \cup \{\{A_1, \ldots, A_n\} \mid (\forall i \in [1, n]) \, A_i \in \mathscr{A} \wedge c_i \in A_i\}$
18: **end for**
19: **return** $\operatorname{argmax}_{S \in \mathscr{S}} cost(S)$

---

sufficient option to harden the network. Although the logic proposition can be derived efficiently, converting it to its DNF may incur into an exponential explosion.

Algorithm $BackwardSearch$ (Algorithm 1) is functionally equivalent to the one described in the previous chapter—in that it generates all possible hardening solutions[3]—under the simplifying hypothesis that initial conditions can be individually disabled, i.e., $(\forall c_i \in C_i)(\exists A \in \mathscr{A})(A = \{c_i\})$. However, our rewriting of the algorithm has several advantages over its original version.

– First, it is more general, as it does not assume that initial conditions can be individually disabled, and incorporates the notions of *allowable action* and *hardening strategy* defined in Sect. 5.3.
– Second, it directly computes a set of possible hardening strategies, rather then a logic proposition that requires additional processing in order to provide actionable intelligence.
– Last, in a time-constrained or real-time scenario where one may be interested in the first available hardening solution, the rewritten algorithm can be easily modified to terminate as soon as a solution is found. To this aim, it is sufficient to change the condition of the main while loop (Line 3) to $(\nexists S \in \mathscr{S})(S \subseteq C_i)$. Such variant of the algorithm will generate hardening strategies that disable initial conditions *closer* to the target conditions.

---

[3]For ease of presentation, the pseudocode of Algorithm 1 does not show how cycles are broken. This is done as in the original algorithm.

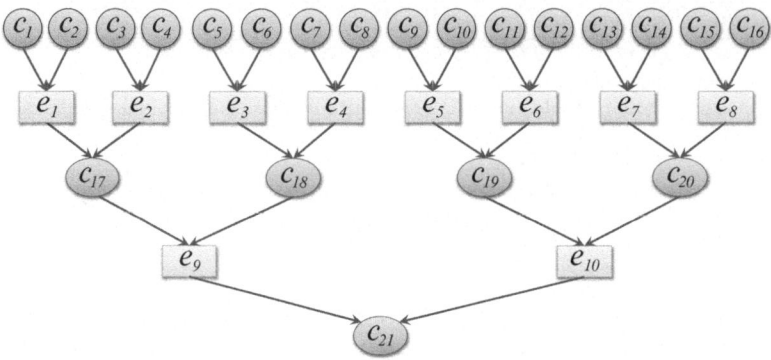

Fig. 5.4 Example of attack graph with $n = 2$ and $d = 4$

However, when used to find the minimum-cost hardening solution, Algorithm $BackwardSearch$ still faces the combinatorial explosion described below. Instead, the algorithm introduced in Sect. 5.4.2 provides a balance between the optimality of the solution and the time to compute it.

Under the simplifying hypothesis that initial conditions can be individually disabled—i.e., $(\forall c_i \in C_i)(\exists A \in \mathscr{A})(A = \{c_i\})$—and allowable actions are pairwise disjoint—i.e., $(\forall A_i, A_j \in \mathscr{A})(A_i \cap A_j = \emptyset)$—it can be proved that, in the worst case, the number of possible hardening strategies is

$$|\mathscr{S}| = |C_t| \cdot n^{\sum_{k=1}^{\frac{d}{2}} n^k} \tag{5.6}$$

and the size of each solution is $n^{\frac{d}{2}}$, where d is the maximum distance (number of edges) between initial and target conditions,[4] and n is the maximum in-degree of nodes in the attack graph. Worst case complexity is then $O(n^{n^d})$.

The previous chapter relies on the assumption that the attack graph of a small and well-protected network is usually small and sparse (the in-degree of each node is small), thus, even if the complexity is exponential, running time should be acceptable in practice. However, the result above shows that computing an optimal solution may be impractical even for relatively small attack graphs. For instance, consider the attack graph of Fig. 5.4, where $n = 2$, $C_t = \{c_{21}\}$, and $d = 4$. According to Eq. (5.6), there are 64 possible hardening strategies in the worst case, each of size 4. The strategy that disables the set of initial conditions $\{c_1, c_3, c_9, c_{11}\}$ is one of such possible strategies. When $d = 6$, the number of initial condition is 64, and the number of possible strategies becomes 16,384. For $d = 8$, $|C_i| = 256$ and the number of possible strategies is over a billion.

---

[4]Note that d is always an even number.

5.4.2 Approximation Algorithm

To address the limitations of the previous network hardening algorithm, we now propose an approximation algorithm that computes reasonably good solutions in a time efficient manner. We will show that, under certain conditions, the solutions computed by the proposed algorithm have a cost that is bound to be within a constant factor of the optimal cost.

Algorithm *ForwardSearch* (Algorithm 2) traverses the attack graph forward, starting from initial conditions. A key advantage of traversing the attack graph forward is that intermediate solutions are indeed network hardening strategies with respect to intermediate conditions. In fact, in a single pass, Algorithm *ForwardSearch* can compute hardening strategies with respect to any condition in C. To limit the exponential explosion of the search space, intermediate solutions can be pruned—based on some pruning strategy—whereas pruning is not possible for the algorithm that traverses the graph backwards. In fact, in this case, intermediate solutions may contain exploits and intermediate conditions, and we cannot say anything about their cost until all the exploits and intermediate conditions have been replaced with sets of initial conditions.

In this section, for ease of presentation, we consider hardening problems with a single target condition. The generalization to the case where multiple target conditions need to be hardened at the same time is straightforward and is discussed below.

Given a set C_t of target conditions, we add a dummy exploit e_i for each condition $c_i \in C_t$, such that e_i has c_i as its only precondition, as shown in Fig. 5.5. Then, we add a dummy target condition c_t, such that all the dummy exploits e_i have c_t are their only postcondition. It is clear that any strategy that hardens the network with respect to c_t implicitly hardens the network with respect to each $c_i \in C_t$. In fact, as c_t is reachable from any dummy exploit e_i, all such exploits need to be prevented, and the only way to achieve this is by disabling the corresponding preconditions, that is hardening the network with respect to all target conditions in C_t.

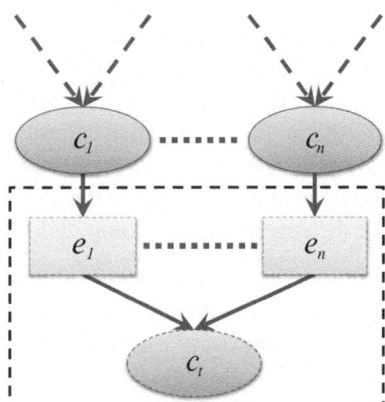

Fig. 5.5 Example of multiple target conditions and dummy target

---

Algorithm 2 $ForwardSearch(G, k)$

Input: Attack graph $G = (E \cup C, R_r \cup R_i)$, and optimization parameter k.
Output: Mapping $\sigma : C \cup E \rightarrow 2^{\mathscr{S}}$, and mapping $minCost : C \cup E \rightarrow \mathbb{R}^+$.
1: $Q \leftarrow TopologicalSort(C \cup E)$
2: **while** $Q \neq \emptyset$ **do**
3:     $q \leftarrow Q.pop()$
4:     **if** $q \in C_i$ **then**
5:         $\sigma(q) \leftarrow \{\{A\} \mid q \in A\}$
6:     **else if** $q \in E$ **then**
7:         $\sigma(q) \leftarrow \bigcup_{c \in C \mid (c,q) \in R_i} \sigma(q)$
8:     **else if** $q \in C \setminus C_i$ **then**
9:         $\{e_1, \ldots, e_m\} \leftarrow \{e \in E \mid (e, q) \in R_i\}$
10:       $\sigma(q) \leftarrow \{S_1 \cup \ldots \cup S_m \mid S_i \in \sigma(e_i)\}$
11:     **end if**
12:    $\sigma(q) \leftarrow topK(\sigma(q), k)$
13:    $minCost(q) = \min_{S \in \sigma(q)} cost(S)$
14: **end while**

Additionally, we assume that, given a target condition c_t, the attack graph is a tree rooted at c_t and having initial conditions as leaf nodes. In Sect. 5.2, we showed an example of how this can be achieved using the mechanism to break cycle adopted by the algorithm discussed in the previous chapter. If the attack graph is not a tree, it can be converted to this form by using such mechanism. Looking at the attack graph from the point of view of a given target condition has the additional advantage of ignoring exploits and conditions that do not contribute to reaching that target condition.

On Line 1, the algorithm performs a topological sort of the nodes in the attack graph (exploits and security conditions), and pushes them into a queue, with initial conditions at the front of the queue. While the queue is not empty, an element q is popped from the queue. If q is an initial condition, then q is associated with a set of strategies $\sigma(q)$ such that each strategy simply contains one of the allowable actions in $\mathscr{A}$ disabling q (Line 5). If q is an exploit, then q is associated with a set of strategies $\sigma(q)$ that is the union of the sets of strategies for each condition c required by q (Line 7). In fact, an exploit can be prevented by disabling any of its required conditions. Finally, if q is an intermediate condition, then q is associated with a set of strategies $\sigma(q)$ such that each strategy is the union of a strategy for each of the exploits that imply q (Lines 9–10). In fact, in order to disable an intermediate condition, all the exploits that imply it must be prevented. When suboptimal solutions are acceptable, then only the best k intermediate solutions are maintained at each step of the algorithm (Line 12), and the minimal hardening cost for the current node is computed accordingly (Line 13).

Example 5.1. Consider the attack graph of Fig. 5.3. The only three allowable actions on the corresponding network are $stop\_ftp(2) = \{ftp(1, 2), ftp(0, 2)\}$, $block\_host(0) = \{ftp(0, 1), sshd(0, 1), ftp(0, 2)\}$, and $stop\_sshd(1) = \{sshd(0, 1)\}$. Assume that $cost(\{stop\_ftp(2)\}) = 20, cost(\{block\_host(0)\}) = 10$, and $cost(\{stop\_sshd(1)\}) = 15$. It is clear that the optimal strategy to harden the network with respect to $root(2)$ is $S = \{block\_host(0)\}$, with a cost of 10. Let us now examine the behavior of the algorithm for $k = 1$. All nodes are added to the queue in topological order, and initial conditions are examined first. After all the initial conditions have been examined, we obtain $\sigma(ftp(1,2)) = \{\{stop\_ftp(2)\}\}$, $\sigma(ftp(0,1)) = \{\{block\_host(0)\}\}$, $\sigma(sshd(0,1)) = \{\{block\_host(0)\}\}$, and $\sigma(ftp(0,2)) = \{\{block\_host(0)\}\}$. Once the algorithm examines exploit $rsh(1,2)$, on Line 7, before pruning, we obtain $\sigma(rsh(1,2)) = \{\{stop\_ftp(2)\}, \{block\_host(0)\}\}$. After pruning (Line 12), we obtain $\sigma(rsh(1,2)) = \{\{block\_host(0)\}\}$, as $\{block\_host(0)\}$ is the strategy with the lowest cost. Finally, we obtain $\sigma(root(2)) = \{\{block\_host(0)\}\}$, that is the algorithm, in this case, returns the optimal solution.

From the example above, it is clear that in our approach administrators only have to assign the cost of performing allowable actions (which are meaningful aggregates of initial conditions), whereas in previous approaches they had to assign cost values to each individual initial condition.

Now, let us consider a different example showing how the value of k may have an impact on the optimality of the solution. Intuitively, the higher the value of k, the closer the computed solution is to the optimal one.

Example 5.2. Consider the attack graph of Fig. 5.6, and assume that $cost(\{A_1\}) = 10$, $cost(\{A_2\}) = 18$, and $cost(\{A_3\}) = 10$. Also assume that cost is additive. It is clear that the optimal strategy to harden the network with respect to c_5 is $S = \{A_2\}$, with a cost of 18. Let us now examine the behavior of the algorithm for $k = 1$. On Line 1 we obtain $Q = \langle c_1, c_2, c_3, c_4, e_1, e_2, c_5 \rangle$. Thus, c_1 is the first node to be examined. After the first four elements of the queue have been examined, we obtain $\sigma(c_1) = \{\{A_1\}\}$, $\sigma(c_2) = \{\{A_2\}\}$, $\sigma(c_3) = \{\{A_2\}\}$, and $\sigma(c_4) = \{\{A_3\}\}$. Then e_1 is considered. The full set of possible strategies for e_1 is $\sigma(e_1) = \{\{A_1\}, \{A_2\}\}$, but, since $k = 1$, only the best one is maintained and propagated to following steps. A similar consideration applies to e_2. In conclusion we obtain $\sigma(e_1) = \{\{A_1\}\}$ $\sigma(e_2) = \{\{A_3\}\}$. Finally, we obtain $\sigma(c_5) = \{\{A_1, A_3\}\}$, and $minCost(c_5) = 20$, which is slightly above the optimal cost. Similarly, it can be shown that, for $k = 2$, the algorithm returns $minCost(c_5) = 18$, i.e., the optimal solution. This confirms that larger values of k make solutions closer to the optimal one.

We now show that, in the worst case—when $k = 1$—the approximation ratio is upper-bounded by $n^{d/2}$. However, experimental results indicate that, in practice, the approximation ratio is much smaller than its theoretical bound. First, let us consider the type of scenario in which solutions may not be optimal. To this aim, consider again the attack graph configuration of Fig. 5.6. When computing solutions for e_1 and e_2 respectively, we make *local* decisions without considering the whole graph, i.e., we independently compute the optimal solution for e_1 and the optimal solution for e_2, given hardening strategies for their preconditions. However, at a later stage, we need to merge solutions for both e_1 and e_2 in order to obtain solutions for c_5. At this point, since there exists an allowable action (i.e., A_2) that would have disabled preconditions of both e_1 and e_2, with a cost lower than the combined cost of their locally optimal solutions, but the strategy including A_2 has been discarded for $k = 1$, the solution is not optimal. This suggests that both k

Fig. 5.6 Example of attack
graph with $d = 2$ and $n = 2$

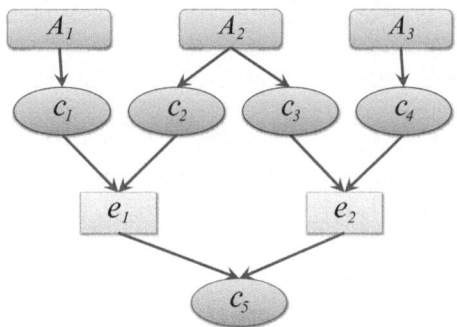

and the maximum in-degree n of nodes in the graph play a role in determining the
optimality of the solution. Additionally, as the algorithm traverses the graph towards
target conditions, there may be a multiplicative effect in the approximation error. In
fact, the depth d of the tree also plays a role in determining the outcome of the
approximation, but this effect can be compensated by increasing the value of k.
We can prove the following theorem.

Theorem 5.1. *Given an attack graph G with depth d and maximum in-degree n,
the upper bound of the approximation ratio of algorithm $ForwardSearch$ for
$k = 1$ is $n^{\frac{d}{2}}$.*

Proof. We prove the result by induction, assuming that the cost function is additive.
We use the term *level l* to denote nodes that are at a distance l from the target
condition. We need to prove that for each $l \in [1, d - 2]$, the cost of hardening
conditions at level l is $n^{\frac{d-l}{2}}$ times the optimal cost. The worst case—depicted in
Fig. 5.7—is the one in which (i) a single allowable action A^* (with $cost(\{A^*\}) = x$)
disables one precondition for each of the $\frac{m}{2}$ exploits $e_{d-1,i}$ at level $d-1$ (i.e., exploits
depending on initial conditions), where $m = n^d$ is the number of initial conditions;
(ii) for each exploit $e_{d-1,i}$, all the preconditions not disabled by A^* are disabled by
an action A_i such that $cost(\{A_i\}) = x - \varepsilon$, where ε is an arbitrarily small positive
real number; and (iii) actions A_i are pairwise disjoint.

Base Case. When choosing a strategy for $e_{d-1,i}$, the algorithm picks the one with
the lowest cost, that is strategy $\{A_i\}$ with cost $x - \varepsilon$. Then, when choosing a strategy
for $c_{d-2,i}$, the algorithm combines strategies for its n predecessors, which all cost
$x - \varepsilon$. Since such strategies are disjoint and cost is additive, the cost to harden any
condition at level $d - 2$ of the attack tree is $n \cdot (x - \varepsilon)$.

Inductive Step. If hardening strategies for conditions at level $d - j$ of the attack
tree cost $n^{j/2} \cdot (x - \varepsilon)$, then hardening strategies for exploits at level $d - j - 1$ of the
attack tree also cost $n^{j/2} \cdot (x - \varepsilon)$. When choosing a strategy for conditions at level
$d - j - 2$, the algorithm combines strategies for its n predecessors, which all cost
$n^{j/2} \cdot (x - \varepsilon)$. Since such strategies are disjoint and cost is additive, the cost to harden
any condition at level $d - j - 2$ of the attack tree is $n \cdot n^{j/2} \cdot (x - \varepsilon) = n^{\frac{j+2}{2}} \cdot (x - \varepsilon)$.
$\square$

Although this result indicates that the bound may increase exponentially with the depth of the attack tree, the bound is in practice—as confirmed by experimental results—much lower than the theoretical bound. In fact, the worst case scenario depicted in Fig. 5.7 is quite unrealistic. Additionally, the bound can be reduced by increasing the value of k. For instance, by setting $k = n$, the bound becomes $n^{\frac{d-2}{2}}$, that is the bound for a graph with depth $d - 2$ and in-degree n.

Fig. 5.7 Worst case scenario

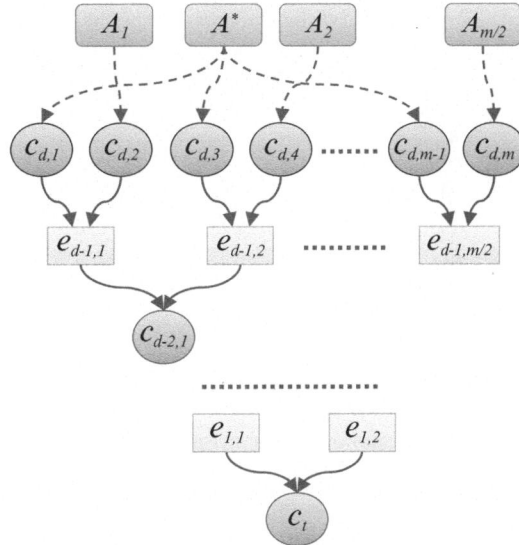

Example 5.3. Consider the attack graph configuration of Fig. 5.6 (with $n = 2$ and $d = 2$), and assume that $cost(\{A_2\}) = x$, $cost(\{A_1\}) = x - \varepsilon$, and $cost(\{A_3\}) = x - \varepsilon$. For $k = 1$, if the cost function is additive, we obtain $minCost(c_5) = 2 \cdot (x - \varepsilon) \approx 2 \cdot x$, which means that in the worst case the cost is twice the optimal cost.

5.5 Experimental Results

In this section, we report the experiments we conducted to validate our approach. Specifically, our objective is to evaluate the performance of algorithm *ForwardSearch* in terms of processing time and approximation ratio for different values of the depth d of the attack graph and the maximum in-degree n of nodes in the graph. In order to obtain graphs with specific values of d and n, we started from realistic graphs, like the one of Fig. 5.3, and augmented them with additional synthetic conditions and exploits. Although the large attack graphs we generated through this process are mostly synthetic, we made considerable efforts to make such graphs consistent with real attack graphs. Additionally, for each such graph, we randomly generated different groupings of initial conditions into allowable actions, in order to account for variability in what administrators can control. All the results reported in this section are averaged over multiple graphs with the same values of d and n, but different configurations of allowable actions.

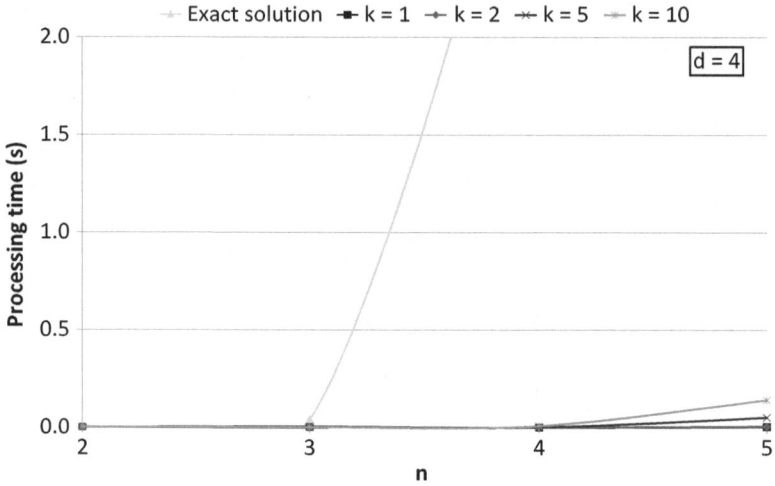

Fig. 5.8 Processing time vs. n for $d = 4$ and different values of k

First, we show that, as expected, computing the optimal solution is feasible only for very small graphs. Figure 5.8 shows how processing time increases when n increases and for $d = 4$, and compares processing times of the exact algorithm with processing times of algorithm $ForwardSearch$ for different values of k. It is clear that the time to compute the exact solution starts to diverge at $n = 4$, whereas processing time of algorithm $ForwardSearch$ is still well under 0.5 s for $k = 10$ and $n = 5$. Similarly, Fig. 5.9 shows how processing time increases when d increases and for $n = 2$, and compares processing times of the exact algorithm with processing times of algorithm $ForwardSearch$ for different values of k. The time to compute the exact solution starts to diverge at $d = 5$, whereas processing time of algorithm $ForwardSearch$ is still under 20 ms for $k = 10$ and $d = 10$.

Figure 5.10 shows how processing time increases when the parameter k increases and for a fixed value of n ($n = 4$) and different values of d. From this chart, it is clear that large graphs can be processed in a few seconds for values of k up to 5. As we will show shortly, relatively small values of k provide a good balance between approximation ratio and processing time, therefore this result is extremely valuable.

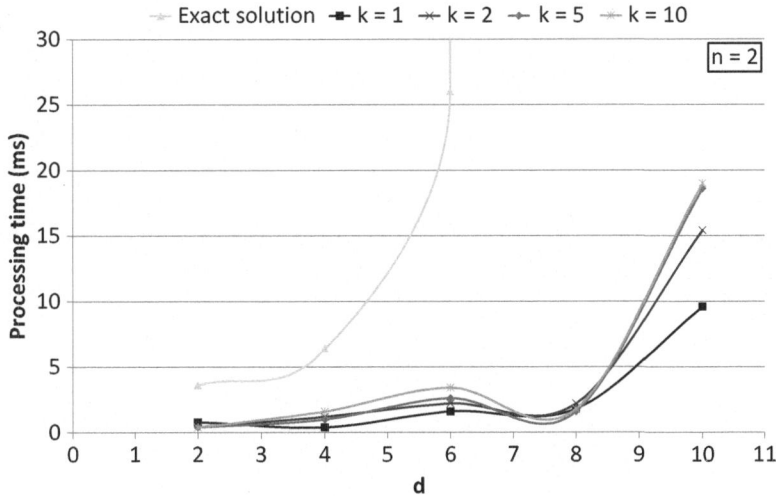

Fig. 5.9 Processing time vs. d for $n = 2$ and different values of k

Similarly, Fig. 5.11 shows how processing time increases when k increases and for a fixed value of d ($d = 8$) and different values of n. This chart confirms that large graphs can be processed in a few seconds for relatively small values of k.

We also observed the relationship between processing time and size of the graphs (in terms of number of nodes). Figure 5.12 shows a scatter plot of average processing times for given pairs of d and n vs. the corresponding graph size. This chart suggests that, in practice, processing time is linear in the size of the graph for small values of k.

Finally, we evaluated the approximation ratio achieved by the algorithm. Figure 5.13 shows how the ratio changes when k increases and for a fixed value of n ($n = 2$) and different values of d. It is clear that the approximation ratio improves when k increases, and, in all cases, the ratio is clearly below the theoretical bound. Additionally, relatively low values of k (between 2 and 6) are sufficient to achieve a reasonably good approximation ratio in a time-efficient manner. Additionally, as observed earlier, processing time is practically linear in the size of the graph for lower values of k. Similarly, Fig. 5.14 shows how the approximation ratio—for a fixed value of d ($d = 4$) and different values of n—improves as k increases. Similar conclusions can be drawn from this chart. In particular, the approximation ratio is always below the theoretical bound.

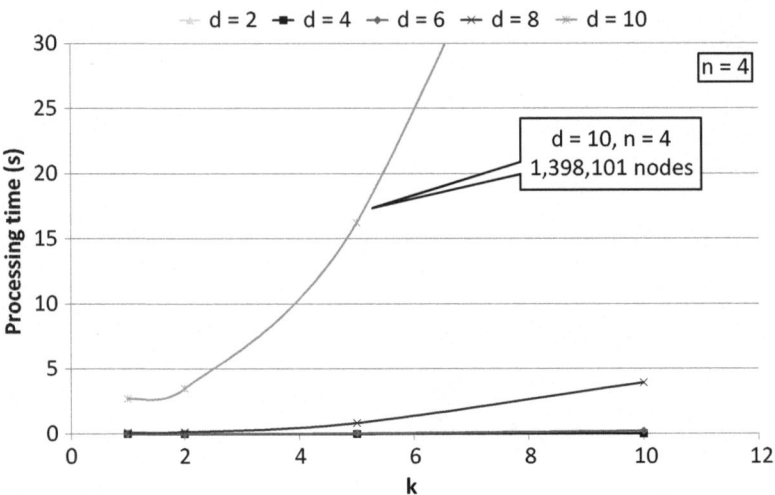

Fig. 5.10 Processing time vs. k for $n = 4$ and different values of d

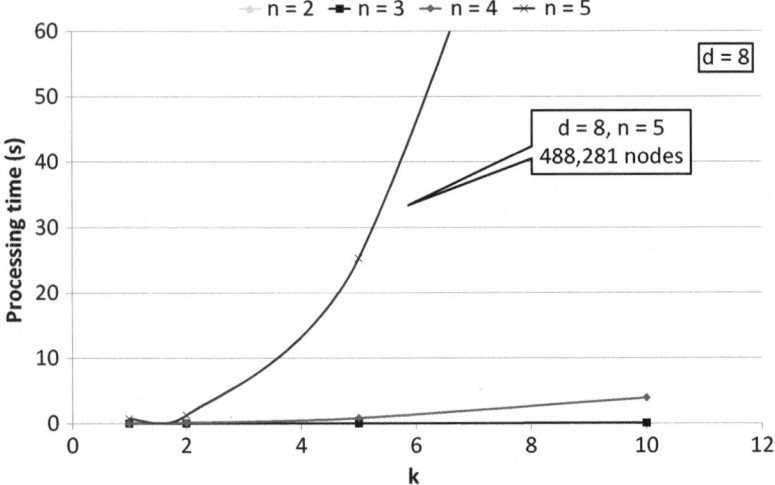

Fig. 5.11 Processing time vs. k for $d = 8$ and different values of n

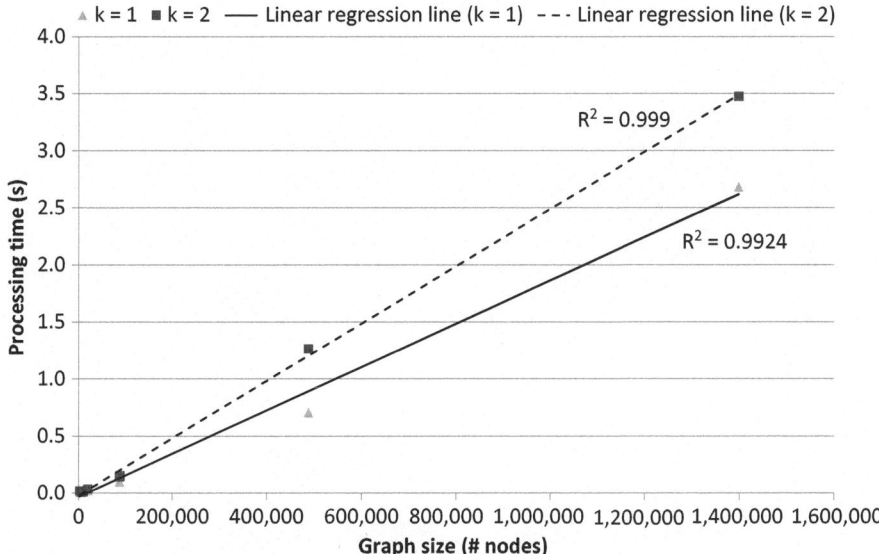

Fig. 5.12 Processing time vs. graph size for different values of k

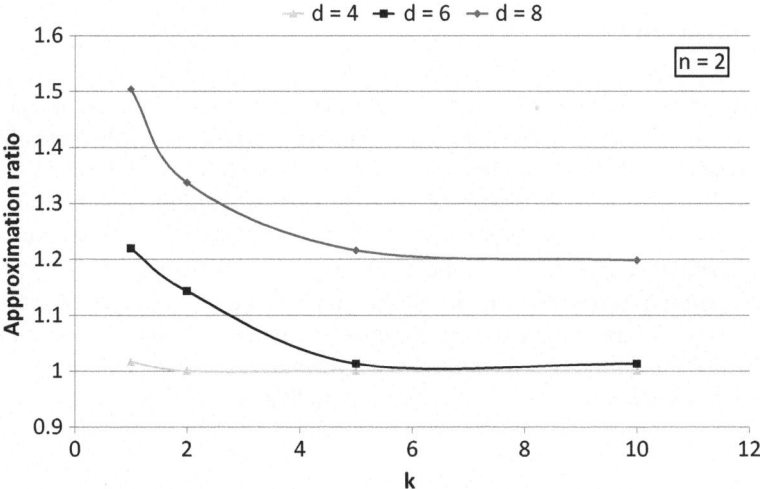

Fig. 5.13 Approximation ratio vs. k for $n = 2$ and different values of d

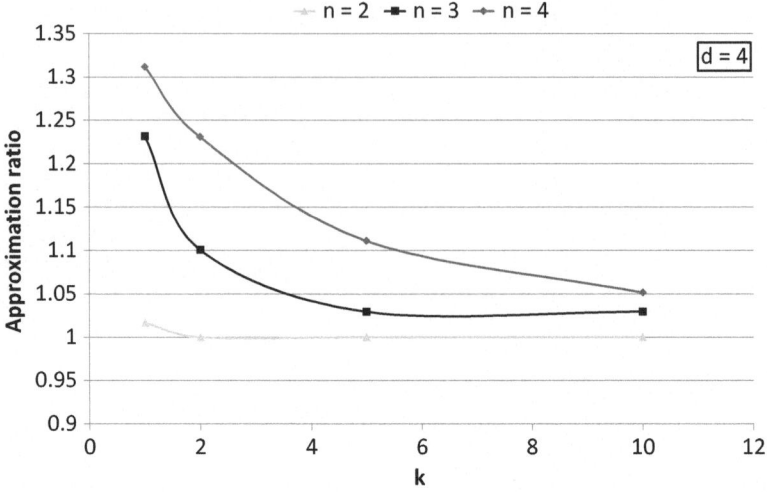

Fig. 5.14 Approximation ratio vs. k for $d = 4$ and different values of n

5.6 Summary

In this chapter, we started by highlighting the limitations of the techniques discussed in the previous chapter. In particular, we showed—both theoretically and
experimentally—that finding the exact solution to this problem is feasible only for
very small graphs. We proposed an approximation algorithm to find reasonably
good solutions in a time-efficient manner. We proved that, under certain reasonable
assumptions, the approximation ratio of this algorithm is bounded by $n^{\frac{d}{2}}$, where n
is the maximum in-degree of nodes in the graph and d is the depth of the graph.
We also showed that, in practice, the approximation ratio is much smaller than its
theoretical bound. Finally, we reported experimental results that confirm the validity
of our approach and motivate further research in this direction.

Reference

1. Steven Noel and Sushil Jajodia. Managing attack graph complexity through visual hierarchical
   aggregation. In *Proceedings of the ACM CCS Workshop on Visualization and Data Mining for
   Computer Security (VizSEC/DMSEC 2004)*, pages 109–118, Fairfax, VA, USA, October 2004.
   ACM.

Chapter 6
Conclusion

In this book, we have reviewed several automated solutions for hardening a network against sophisticated multi-step intrusions. After reviewing necessary background information, we described a network hardening technique for automatically generating hardening solutions comprised of only initial conditions. Such a solution was more enforceable than previous approaches that aim to break attack paths. After discussing limitations of this approach, including the complexity issue and the assumption of independent initial conditions, we then pursued an improved heuristic technique to remove such an assumption and to achieve a near-optimal approximation while scaling linearly with the size of the inputs. We have validated the performance of this approach through experiments conducted on synthetic yet realistic attack graphs.

Our future plans include evaluating the proposed approach on real data as well as deepening our understanding of cost functions. Although additional work is required, the theoretical and experimental results obtained so far are very promising, and the proposed algorithm could be easily adopted to augment the hardening capabilities currently offered by available commercial tools such as Cauldron [1], a vulnerability analysis framework originally developed by members of our research group. Cauldron's current approach to optimal network hardening is based on disabling the smallest possible set of edges in the attack graph, in order to prevent the attacker from reaching certain target conditions. However, this approach has the same limitations of selectively removing exploits. As we discussed earlier in the book, it is not always possible to remove arbitrary exploits (or attack paths) without removing their causes, whereas removing sets of independent initial conditions will be easier to enforce. We plan to integrate the hardening approaches described in this book into Cauldron and evaluate the end product against real world networks and hardening requirements.

L. Wang et al., *Network Hardening: An Automated Approach to Improving Network Security*, SpringerBriefs in Computer Science, DOI 10.1007/978-3-319-04612-9_6, © The Author(s) 2014

Reference

1. Sushil Jajodia, Steven Noel, Pramod Kalapa, Massimiliano Albanese, and John Williams. Cauldron: Mission-centric cyber situational awareness with defense in depth. In *Proceedings of the Military Communications Conference (MILCOM 2011)*, pages 1339–1344, Baltimore, MD, USA, November 2011.